"Mirror, mirror on the wall who's the fittest of them all? Ok, so we don't ask that when we look in a mirror, but we are guilty of looking to it for validation of our fitness markers. Forward thinking fitness understands that the mirror can lie. Bulk, curves, and cuts aren't enough to overcoming fear, depression, and self-sabotaging insecurities. There is a very spiritual side to being physically fit. Through *Virtuosity*, Donavan DeGrie and Brian Mills empower and inspire such a radical transformation that you'll look in the mirror and see someone full of vitality on the inside."
TONY NOLAN, *Speaker and Author*

"We live in a world in desperate need of men, and in particular, men of God. But you do not microwave a boy into a man; it takes time, leadership, and discipline. My friends Brian Mills and Donavan DeGrie have written a helpful work in *Virtuosity* to help young men become men of God. I commend this book—Dads, mentors, student pastors, and young men, read this one!"
DR. ALVIN L. REID, *Professor of Evangelism and Student Ministry/*
Bailey Smith Chair of Evangelism, Southeastern Baptist Theological Seminary,
Wake Forest, North Carolina

"Growing in one's faith is not merely acquiring more knowledge about God. Instead, it is our ability to be devoted to basic principles of God's Word and apply those timeless truths to our lives. In *Virtuosity* you will find a desire to 'do the common uncommonly well.' Join authors Donavan DeGrie and Brian Mills in a 40-day journey that focuses on a 'quality' walk with God. More is not always better, and those who grow in their faith are often committed to pursuing God with intentionality and intensity."
CLAYTON KING, *Founder of Clayton King Ministries*

"For many guys the thought of being spiritually fit often seems complicated and out of reach. Brian Mills and Donavan DeGrie have put together a 40 day journey that focuses and coaches you through a daily developing walk with Jesus that moves you toward spiritual maturity. Virtuosity is a must read that is life changing."
SEAN MILLS, Next Generation Pastor, theChurch.at Tulsa, OK

"*Virtuosity* is a challenge all men need to take. As I work with students and leaders across the country, I recognize more and more the importance of excellence and living our lives for Christ to the fullest. *Virtuosity* challenges guys to do this very thing. Day by day you will dive into Scripture, be challenged, and then be given some practical solutions on how to accomplish the challenge of that day. I would encourage all ministries to use this resource as a part of the guy discipleship."
Clint Ivy, Youth Pastor, Prestonwood Baptist Church

VIRTUOSITY

—— DOING THE COMMON **UNCOMMONLY WELL** ——

LifeWay Press®
Nashville, Tennessee

ISBN: 978-1-4300-3980-8
Item: 005720882

Dewey Decimal Classification Number: 248.83
Subject Heading: MEN/CHRISTIAN LIFE/MASCULINITY

Printed in the United States of America

Student Ministry Publishing
LifeWay Church Resources
One LifeWay Plaza
Nashville, TN 37234-0144

We believe that the Bible has God for its author; salvation for its end;
and truth, without any mixture of error, for its matter
and that all Scripture is totally true and trustworthy.
To review LifeWay's doctrinal guideline,
please visit *www.lifeway.com/doctrinalguideline*.

CONTENTS

ABOUT THE WRITERS

BRIAN MILLS is the Executive Ministries and Teaching Pastor at Englewood Baptist Church in Jackson, TN. Before taking the role of Executive Pastor, he spent 14 years serving in full time student ministry. After graduating from Ouachita Baptist University, he has led student ministries as small as 7 and as large as 2,000 students. He is currently a speaker and consultant for churches and ministries all over the United States. Brian is also the co-author of *Checkpoints - A Tactical Guide to Manhood*. Brian is passionate about seeing people saved, baptized, and growing in their faith, along with equipping and leading the staff and volunteers where he is currently serving. He is married to Jennifer Mills, co-author of *Salvaging My Identity* and father to McKenna and Parker.

DONAVAN DEGRIE is currently a CrossFit Seminar Staff instructor and employed by CrossFit Headquarters. His job includes traveling the world and teaching others the methodologies of CrossFit. As one of CrossFit's top coaches, he has the pleasure of instructing anywhere from 40-60 people about CrossFit every week. He has personally impacted thousands of lives through their health and fitness. Donavan enjoys being an ambassador for CrossFit and sharing the truth about how to live a healthy lifestyle. At the same time, Donavan understands that his greatest calling in this lifetime is to be an ambassador for Christ. *Therefore, we are ambassadors for Christ, God making his appeal through us. We implore you on behalf of Christ, be reconciled to God* (2 Cor. 5:20, ESV). His passion for CrossFit and sharing God's truth has lead him to partner up with Brian Mills in writing *Virtuosity*. Donavan desires to use the opportunity that God has given him to help others through improving their fitness, and when given the right opportunity, to share the hope that he has found through Christ. Donavan's goal is to strive to do the "commonly uncommonly well" in every aspect of his life.

FOREWORD

Virtuosity is doing the common uncommonly well. I have found this to hold true in my CrossFit® career as well as in my faith. Very often it is the most simplistic mechanics and disciplines that produce the best results. Focusing on the basics has allowed me to achieve great things in the CrossFit community and grow in my faith. I am often reminded of the simple truth that spiritual growth comes from spending time in God's Word, praying, and accountability. I am thankful that God has allowed me to use my giftedness for His glory. I believe that virtuosity is something that we can pursue in every aspect of our lives. This book takes God's basic and timeless truths and puts them into practical application. Virtuosity is something that I pursue as a husband, father, coach, athlete, and follower of Christ.

RICH FRONING
FOUR-TIME CROSSFIT GAMES CHAMPION

INTRODUCTION

While personal perfection may be desired, it is unattainable on earth. Only one man has lived and never sinned: Jesus. The Bible says we have a High Priest (Jesus) *who in every respect has been tempted as we are, yet without sin* (Heb. 4:15, ESV). And 2 Corinthians 5:21 says, *He made the One who did not know sin to be sin for us, so that we might become the righteousness of God in Him.* And again, describing Jesus in 1 Peter 2:22: *And no deceit was found in His mouth.* Perfection has been achieved by one. Yet we read Jesus' challenge in Matthew 5:48: *Be perfect, therefore, as your heavenly Father is perfect.* Jesus set a standard that no one can achieve but all should strive for. This can become frustrating in your walk with Christ. Paul wrote of this struggle in Romans 7:18, *For I know that nothing good dwells in me, that is, in my flesh. For I have the desire to do what is right, but not the ability to carry it out* (ESV). Virtuosity is not about being perfect; it is simply about the challenge to do the common uncommonly well. It assists you on your journey to live out 1 Peter 1:16, *Be holy, because I am holy.*

Few can tell you how to calculate a gymnastics score. But most can tell you that the highest score is a 10 and the lowest score is a 0. In gymnastics only 9.7 points can be awarded for a flawless routine. The last 0.3 points is awarded for virtuosity. Virtuosity is only rewarded to those gymnasts who do the common uncommonly well. CrossFit founder and CEO Greg Glassman describes it this way: "Unlike risk and originality, virtuosity is elusive, supremely elusive. It is, however, readily recognized by the audience as well as by the coach and the athlete. There is a compelling tendency among novices developing any skill or art, whether learning to play the violin, write poetry, or compete in gymnastics, to quickly move past the fundamentals and on to more elaborate, more sophisticated movements, skills, or techniques."[1]

Often we believe that getting to heaven means we must impress God. We forget the truth of Ephesians 2:8, *For it is by grace you have been saved, through faith—and this is not from yourselves, it is the gift of God* (NIV). Regardless of our work ethic, we will never work enough to impress God or get ourselves to heaven. Virtuosity is not about working harder to win points with Christ; it is about living a life of obedience with complete devotion to our Lord. It is about doing the common uncommonly well.

Virtuosity has been adopted by CrossFit. Glassman again stated, "The first and most important component of beginning CrossFit is to follow our charter of mechanics, consistency, and then intensity. These three aspects are intricately interrelated; CrossFit does not work to its potential unless you execute each one and understand how it is bound to the others." When a client walks into a gym, the goal is to educate them on this concept of mechanics (technique), consistency (proper form over numerous reps and training a neurological pattern of familiarity with the movements), and finally intensity (pushing yourself to your personal limitations). The goal is to achieve personal intensity in every workout, but the journey to get there is not as quick as some would like it to be. "Intensity," as Glassman states, "is the independent variable most commonly associated with the rate of return on favorable adaptation. More simply put, intensity brings about all the good results from working out. However, we also have to realize that intensity is relative to our physical and psychological tolerances. This is a process, and one that takes an indeterminate amount of time, so be patient. No one ever got in shape overnight."

The journey to spiritual maturity is similar. It will require patience and trust in God. Many will strive to do more to "impress" God, but that will be destructive. More is not better. Better is better. A quality walk with God requires a firm understanding of the basic mechanics (humility, quality vs. quantity, discipline, grace, discipleship, the battle within, relationships, and attitude). Once the basic mechanics have been rooted, then there will be a transition to consistency. Consistency in this book refers to the practical applications of mechanics. For example, a person may have an understanding of how to be humble but fail to exercise that mechanic of humility in daily life. Knowing the right things to say, but never fully living it out. Jesus spoke to this in John 5:39-40: *You pore over the Scriptures because you think you have eternal life in them, yet they testify about Me. And you are not willing to come to Me so that you many have life.* Ever met someone who knows fitness yet refuses to work out? Or the guy who talks a lot about Christianity but his walk shows no evidence of faith? The goal is to grow in your understanding of the proper mechanics so you can become consistent in applying those concepts to your life. Understanding the mechanics and consistent application will help you achieve the last component of spiritual growth: intensity. Intensity means waking up every day with a desire to give your best to Christ as you embrace forgiveness in your shortcomings. Some days will be better than others, but the goal does not change: *Therefore, whether you eat or drink, or whatever you do, do everything for God's glory* (1 Cor. 10:31).

How does that apply to our spiritual journey? Throughout the book you will hear the concept of mechanics, consistency, and intensity. Similar to fitness, the goal is to achieve intensity. Remember that intensity is personal and different for every single person. Rich Froning, a four-time CrossFit Games champion, has a radically different personal intensity than 99 percent of the fitness population. But just because you can't do the same workout as Rich in the same amount of time, doesn't mean you should quit working out. Fitness and spiritual maturity is a process, and they were designed to meet you where you are. Do not compare yourself to the people around you. Rather, look to Christ as the standard. No one is perfect, but choose to give your best (intensity) every single day.

Not that I have already reached the goal or am already fully mature, but I make every effort to take hold of it because I also have been taken hold of by Christ Jesus. Brothers, I do not consider myself to have taken hold of it. But one thing I do: Forgetting what is behind and reaching forward to what is ahead, I pursue as my goal the prize promised by God's heavenly call in Christ Jesus. —Philippians 3:12-14

Each week we will target one of eight virtues with the intent of pursuing virtuosity. As you read in the introduction, virtuosity is a term coined by gymnastics that CrossFit has adopted. It means to do the common uncommonly well. Each virtue we cover features a daily Scripture passage, followed by a challenge. Then each day ends with a Consistency challenge. The Consistency challenge is a guide that gives you a few steps on how to accomplish the daily challenge. Each week will end with a day titled "Intensity." This is a day for you to reflect on what you have read the past five days. The Intensity section includes review questions from each day. The goal of both the Consistency and Intensity sections is to practically apply what you have learned from the previous week.

Virtuosity is a book that is designed for you to go through by yourself or with a band of brothers. The challenge is for you to commit to reading five days a week, for eight weeks. At the end of the fifth day, we want you to meet with the group that has accepted the 40 day challenge with you. The focus of this weekly meeting is to go through the Intensity section together. Openly discuss what you have learned from each day. Talk about the challenges of living out these virtues. Use the review questions provided as a way to hold each other accountable. Men need accountability and *Virtuosity* is designed to help you take that step. Proverbs 27:17 says, *Iron sharpens iron, and one man sharpens another.* We need people in our lives who sharpen us. *Virtuosity* helps you get sharpened if you follow the charter.

Like Brian referred to in his book *Checkpoints: A Tactical Guide to Manhood,* "The eight subjects in this study are not meant to be an exhaustive treatment on the complexities of maturing into manhood, but in our experience they are the primary chisels that shape what type of men the next generation will be." We don't want you simply to think right about the topics in this book, we want to give you tools to live by. We want to take a lot of complex topics that all guys face on a day-to-day basis and challenge you in a simplistic way to live them out. To do the common (everyday tasks) uncommonly well, we must live out a more committed life.

This eight week journey will allow you to practically apply the commandments and virtues that God has called us to through His Word. However, this is not a list of "do's" for you in your Christian walk. It is simply a guide for you to use as you continue your walk with Christ. So enlist a band of brothers and choose to start the journey today. Set a weekly meeting where you will discuss the book over the next eight weeks and commit to the 40 day journey of doing the common uncommonly well.

Added feature: Go to *lifeway.com/virtuosity* for free downloadable videos featuring workouts with four-time CrossFit champion, Rich Froning, and session introductions with author and CrossFit Seminar Staff, Donavan DeGrie.

MECHANICS OF HUMILITY

DAY I MECHANICS OF HUMILITY
ACCOMPLISHMENTS

Have this mind among yourselves, which is yours in Christ Jesus, who, though he was in the form of God, did not count equality with God a thing to be grasped, but emptied himself, by taking the form of a servant, being born in the likeness of men. —Philippians 2:5-7 (ESV)

In Philippians 2, Paul does an excellent job of describing humility. Jesus was and forever will be the standard for humility. Many people tend to boast in their accomplishments and what they have achieved in this lifetime. But when those accomplishments are compared to the cross, they don't even begin to come close. Christ came and reconciled humanity back to God. What have you accomplished in this lifetime that can compare to what Christ accomplished over 2,000 years ago?

Rich Froning finished second at the CrossFit Games in 2010. Most would have been pleased with that accomplishment, but not Rich. He was always striving to be better and to push himself to his personal limitations (intensity). His second-place finish fell short of what he wanted to accomplish and brought him to a season of searching for truth. The next three months would be a pivotal transition in Rich's life and a new motivation for why he wanted to compete and what it was he wanted to accomplish. He would get a tattoo on his side that would remind him of his purpose:

But far be it from me to boast except in the cross of our Lord Jesus Christ, by which the world has been crucified to me, and I to the world —Galatians 6:14 (ESV)

Rich is a very talented person, and no one has come close to accomplishing what he has in the CrossFit realm. The best way I can describe it is to say that Rich is to CrossFit as Michael Jordan is to basketball. Not just a four-time champion, but also a person who has helped redefine fitness and put CrossFit on the map. Rich is the face of the sport. But Rich understands that nothing he accomplishes in this lifetime will even begin to come close to the cross. When his journey is finished and he meets God face-to-face, he is not going to boast about his accomplishments in this lifetime. Rather, he is going to say that he has nothing to boast about except for what Christ has accomplished. There is nothing wrong with achieving great things in this lifetime, but the big question is *what are you doing with that platform?* Are you going to make much of Christ or of yourself?

Accomplishments are not bad. Achieving goals that we have set is a beautiful thing. Most people do not achieve great things in this lifetime because they lack drive and discipline, or because they quit when things get difficult. Later chapters in this book will address those mechanics and how they are essential in transforming boys into biblical men of God.

God has gifted each and every one of us to do great things, but do we find more value in the gift or the Giver? Will we make much of ourselves or of Christ?

We must be careful to not become prideful or arrogant as we achieve goals we have set for ourselves. How do you know if you are becoming increasingly focused on yourself or your accomplishments?

1) When talking to other people, do you spend more of your time talking about your accomplishments or genuinely getting to know the person you are talking to?

2) When meeting someone new, do you feel the need to define yourself by something you have accomplished?

It is okay for your accomplishments to come to light, but do you feel the need to let people know what you have accomplished when first meeting them?

3) Do you spend more time reflecting on your accomplishments or on what Christ has already accomplished?

Achieving great things in this lifetime can be a God-glorifying thing. But if our driving force is to make much of ourselves instead of Christ, then we will never find true joy or be able to use those accomplishments for His glory. We must follow the words of John the Baptist: *He must increase, but I must decrease* (John 3:30).

✪ CONSISTENCY ———

1) Viewing Christ. How do you view Christ in your life? Do you reflect upon the gospel on a daily basis? Are you memorizing God's Word and understanding the full depth of what Jesus has already accomplished?

Take the time every day this week to reflect on what Christ has accomplished. A great place to start is by reading Philippians 2. Strive to memorize Philippians 2:5-7.

2) Viewing yourself. Take an honest assessment of yourself today. When having a conversation with others, do you tend to spend the majority of time talking about yourself or sharing your accomplishments? If this is the case, begin the conversation asking questions about the other person. Desire just to spend quality time getting to know him or her. This will take patience and humility. In return, those you meet will probably ask questions about you and you will still have the opportunity to boast about what Christ has accomplished in and through your life.

3) Viewing others. When viewing others, do you tend to make much of their accomplishments? When someone shares he made an "A" on an exam or did something great, do you genuinely congratulate him? Or do you immediately try to one-up him? Build others up and rejoice in their accomplishments.

DAY 2 MECHANICS OF HUMILITY
SELF-EVALUATION

Search me, O God, and know my heart! Try me and know my thoughts! And see if there be any grievous way in me, and lead me in the way everlasting! —Psalm 139:23-24 (ESV)

C. J. Mahaney sums it up best by saying, "Humility is honestly assessing ourselves in light of God's holiness and our sinfulness."[2] How we view ourselves will reveal our hearts. The gap perceived between God's holiness and our sinfulness will reveal our understanding of humility. If the gap is small, then we either see ourselves too highly or we are nullifying God's significance. Neither of which is a desired outcome if we are pursuing humility. In the journey of mortifying pride in our lives, we must constantly examine our sinfulness in light of God's holiness. The two are inseparable.

There is a four-step process in clearly evaluating ourselves. The goal of this four-step process is to help us view God and ourselves through the right lenses, so that we can pursue humility. The first step is viewing God's holiness on a daily basis through His Word.

1) God is holy. Reflect on these verses: *There is none holy like the LORD: for there is none besides you; there is no rock like our God* (1 Sam. 2:2, ESV). *Holy, holy, holy is the LORD of hosts; the whole earth is full of his glory* (Isa. 6:3, ESV).

There are hundreds of passages that describe God's character, but most of them sum it up in one word—*holy*. Holy means to be set apart and unlike anything else. It is the crowning aspect of God's character. Isaiah saw God's presence and experienced the Seraphim proclaiming, "Holy, holy, holy." Notice the heavenly beings weren't declaring "Good, good, good," or "Loving, loving loving." Repetition is used for emphasis and importance in Scripture. "Holy, holy, holy" is the only three-fold character description for God in the Bible.

The second step is understanding the standard God has called us to.

2) God's standard. God's standard is high: *You therefore must be perfect, as your heavenly Father is perfect* (Matt. 5:48, ESV). In most schools, 70 percent is a passing score and anything less is considered failure. But in life, without a scale or standard, there is no way of evaluating performance. Performance, whether in the gym, at work, or spiritually speaking, has to be based on some type of standard. God's standard, however, is perfection. You either make a 100 or you fail. There is nothing in between.

3) Self-evaluation. This is the focus of the day. We must clearly understand how we stack up to God's standard. We can only have a clear view of ourselves when we have a clear view of God's holiness and the standard He has called us to. Evaluating ourselves without the standard of God will only cause us to have a distorted view of ourselves.

We need to clearly understand Paul's words in Romans 3: *None is righteous, no, not one; no one understands; no one seeks for God. All have turned aside; together they have become worthless; no one does good, not even one* (Rom. 3:10-12, ESV). God is perfect, but we are far from perfection.

Sometimes I fight the tendency to falsely evaluate my fitness. I think I am training hard and becoming more fit. But the moment I do a workout with Rich, I am instantly reminded of why he is a champion. If you ever start feeling great about your spiritual accomplishments, stack yourself against the best: Jesus. Your view of yourself will change drastically.

4) Christ is the gap. *Therefore, if anyone is in Christ, he is a new creation. The old has passed away; behold, the new has come* (2 Cor. 5:17, ESV). Remember the gap that was referred to at the beginning of the day? When we truly grasp the chasm between God's holiness and our sinfulness, humility will flood through us. The beauty is that gap has been filled through Christ. Only through a clear view of the gospel can we understand that we don't live up to the standard God has called us to. If we fail to recognize this, then we will make failing steps to minimize the gap. Our futile striving will cause us to think highly of ourselves instead of Christ.

We have a choice to either make much of ourselves or make much of Christ. The two conflict. You cannot have both. In order to grow in humility we must have a clear view of ourselves in light of God's holiness. Without an honest view of ourselves, it will become impossible to live a humble lifestyle.

⊗ CONSISTENCY ———

1) Spend time in God's Word. Reflect over the passages that were covered today, and begin to use the four-step process of growing in humility.

2) Pray. Begin to pray that God would give you a correct view of yourself in light of His holiness. Humble yourself before Him and thank Him for making you worthy through Christ.

3) Make Christ your standard. Take the same mind-set of Paul in saying: *For I am the least of the apostles, unworthy to be called an apostle, because I persecuted the church of God. But by the grace of God I am what I am, and his grace toward me was not in vain. On the contrary, I worked harder than any of them, though it was not I, but the grace of God that is with me* (1 Cor. 15:9-10, ESV). Paul had a clear view of his sinfulness and compared it to God's grace. The goal of this is not to put yourself down, but to honestly evaluate yourself.

DAY 3 MECHANICS OF HUMILITY
ENTITLEMENT

For by the grace given me I say to every one of you: Do not think of yourself more highly than you ought, but rather think of yourself with sober judgment, in accordance with the faith God has distributed to each of you. —Romans 12:3 (NIV)

It is no stretch to say that guys love to think highly of themselves. Through the years, guys have become more and more focused on themselves. A narcissistic worldview has been adopted by guys and the result of a narcissistic worldview always leads to an entitled man.

The disciples even battled narcissism. We read in Luke 9:46: *An argument started among the disciples as to which of them would be the greatest* (NIV). They turned on each other and battled over who was going to be the top dog. They started thinking too much of themselves. Jesus' words to His disciples that day hold true for His disciples of this day: *For it is one who is least among you all who is the greatest* (Luke 9:48, NIV). Yet narcissistic, audacious claims come out of our mouths all the time. "I deserve to be the leader on this team!" "My parents should respect me more!" "I should have been hired for that position!" "My parents owe this to me!" "Doesn't she know who I am?" "I can't believe my teacher gave me that grade. Wait until my parents get a hold of her!" We feel so entitled that our focus is on receiving rather than giving. The problem is we really believe we deserve "it." We have lost the servant heart of biblical manhood. This sense of entitlement keeps us from being humble men of God. Entitlement keeps us from doing the common, uncommonly well.

The following story is the epitome of entitlement.

In the spring of 2014, an 18 year old high school girl in New Jersey filed suit against her parents, demanding they continue to pay for her private school education, impending college costs, and lawyer fees, despite moving out of their home. She claimed her parents tossed her out, while her parents say she left voluntarily because she refused to live by the rules of their home, including not doing chores, being disrespectful, not abiding by curfew, and not following their direction about a boyfriend relationship. She moved in with a friend and took legal action. She later dropped the lawsuit and moved back home after the judge took a dim view of her claim. "Have you ever in your experience seen such gross disrespect for a parent? I don't see it in my house," Family Division Judge Peter Bogaard said at the hearing.[3]

I often watch athletes quit teams because they feel their coaches don't treat them the way they should be treated. Or they quit because they were not given the position they thought they deserved. I watch college graduates turn down jobs that could take them to CEO positions in the future simply because they think they should be a CEO now. These are clear pictures of entitlement.

We must remember, a prideful heart will lead to our downfall as leaders. Proverbs 16:18 tells us that pride comes before the fall. Pride causes entitlement to rise up in us. Paul addressed this issue with the Corinthian church in 1 Corinthians 4:6-13. The Corinthian Christians were becoming very prideful and entitled. Paul warned the Corinthian Christians about moving away from the Scriptures to justify their sense of entitlement. 1 Corinthians 4:6 says: *Now, brothers, I have applied these things to myself and Apollos for your benefit, so that you may learn from us the saying: 'nothing beyond what is written.' The purpose is that none of you will be inflated with pride in favor of one person over another.*

We can't justify our sense of entitlement. We must pause and recognize who we are in Christ and who Christ has called us to be. Paul clearly understood his place: *Even now, we are like the world's garbage, like the dirt everyone scrapes off their sandals* (1 Cor. 4:13b). Paul recognized that he was nothing without Christ. In the same way, we are nothing without Christ, and we are certainly not entitled to anything. For us as men, to do the common uncommonly well, we must tackle our pride and our sense of entitlement.

✪ CONSISTENCY: ────

1. Start each day spending time with God. Every day is a battle, and that battle begins from within. We need to begin the day with a desire and mind-set to imitate Christ. As Ephesians 5:1 says: *Therefore be imitators of God, as beloved children* (ESV).

2. Memorize Scripture that will equip you when facing temptations. We are all tempted with this issue of entitlement in different ways. Scripture tells us that our enemy is *like a roaring lion, seeking someone to devour* (1 Pet. 5:8, ESV). He attacks us where we are weak. Evaluate your weaknesses. How are you being attacked? Find Scripture that speaks to that issue and memorize it. For example, if you're battling lust, an appropriate passage might be Job 31:1: *I made a covenant with my eyes not to look lustfully at a young woman* (NIV). Let God's Word sink deeply into your heart so that when the attack comes, you have truth to stand on.

3. Evaluate your perspective on things. I like to say you need to recognize your blessings. All too often we think we deserve something when really all we deserve is death due to our sinful nature. Remember you're blessed, so be a blessing to others and pay it forward. When you think like a servant, you lead like a servant. When you lead like a servant, you act more like Christ.

DAY 4 MECHANICS OF HUMILITY
GRATEFULNESS

Give thanks in all circumstances; for this is God's will for you in Christ Jesus. —1 Thessalonians 5:18 (NIV)

Gratefulness is not a character trait that most guys embody or desire. However those who are grateful have a clear understanding of God's grace in their lives. We must maintain a heart of gratitude even when life does not turn out the way we want it to. Few people reflect this truth better than former Buffalo Bills quarterback Jim Kelly.

Mr. Kelly took his team to the Super Bowl® four years in a row and lost every single time! In 2000, his hunting trip in Alaska ended in a plane crash into 39-degree water. He had to kick out the window and swim to the surface just to stay alive. When he was 37 his dream came true of having his first son. Eight years later, his son passed away from Krabbe disease. To top it all off, he was diagnosed with cancer in 2013. This led him to have multiple surgeries and suffer great pain. Through all of this, Jim, now age 54, said to Rick Reilly in an *ESPN.com* article, "I've been blessed ... I wouldn't change a thing."[4] When you suffer, self-pity and frustration is a lot easier to fall into than gratefulness. A grateful heart is cultivated in the valley. 1 Thessalonians 5:18 says: *Give thanks in all circumstances; for this is God's will for you in Christ Jesus* (NIV).

Gratefulness keeps you grounded and allows you to remember where you came from. So often we see celebrities or athletes rise to stardom and watch them become self-absorbed people. They focus on themselves and their natural abilities and talents, forgetting that they are blessed by such opportunities.

I have watched middle school athletes make it into high school and become "famous." I have watched some become five-star athletes who then forgot where they came from. Success can be a huge barrier to gratefulness. When you focus completely on your success without reflecting on how you arrived there, you're prone to take credit for your accomplishments and bask in your success. The heart of gratitude is lost.

When Paul says *give thanks in all circumstances,* he means all...the good, the bad, and the ugly! Gratefulness is an attitude of the heart that only a devoted follower of Christ can achieve. Sometimes we have to dig deep to be grateful for our circumstances. When we come to the realization that we are nothing more than sinners saved by the grace of God, then our circumstances won't seem quite as significant.

I love how Edward Mote, the author of the great hymn "The Solid Rock," words it:

> *My hope is built on nothing less*
> *Than Jesus' blood and righteousness.*
> *I dare not trust the sweetest frame,*
> *But wholly trust in Jesus' Name.*
> *On Christ the solid Rock I stand,*
> *All other ground is sinking sand;*
> *All other ground is sinking sand.*

When life is high or when life is low, do we find our gratefulness in Jesus Christ alone?

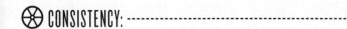

CONSISTENCY:

1. Count your blessings. Consider for a moment where you are, your accomplishments, and your blessings. Turn your attention to God and give Him thanks for all He has done in and through you.

2. Reflect on the hymn. Go back to the hymn "The Solid Rock," and read it three more times. Thank God that your hope rests on Him.

3. Express your gratefulness. Write out five things in your life that you are grateful for no matter what you are going through. Pray a prayer of thanksgiving for those five things. Remember God uses the journey to cultivate a grateful heart in us.

DAY 5 MECHANICS OF HUMILITY
TALENT

Every good gift and every perfect gift is from above, coming down from the Father of lights with whom there is no variation of shadow due to change —James 1:17 (ESV)

Kevin Durant, One of the most talented players in the NBA, has said, "I know that the hard work got me here. And the day I stop working hard, this can all go away."[5] Kevin Durant did not become one of the best players in the NBA by pure luck. He made a daily decision to better himself. When asked after a game how he continues to average over 30 points a game, he said, "Thank God, that's all I can say. Jesus Christ."[6] Some people may find his answer to be cheesy, but I truly believe that he was giving credit back to God for his talents. When others inquire about your natural giftedness, what is your response? Is it prideful and self-rooted, or do you give the credit back to God?

It is easy to give God credit when we know that we could not have achieved something without Him. We didn't have the talent or ability to pull it off, but God came through. On the opposite end, it is extremely difficult to give God the glory in areas we are gifted in. You don't always hear a post-game interview similar to Kevin Durant's, where someone gives sincere credit to God. A lot of times, the opposite is true in professional sports. NFL cornerback Richard Sherman has been quoted many times saying that he is the best cornerback of the league. Now, I am not trying to downplay the fact that Sherman is a very talented individual. His team won the Super Bowl® in 2014, and he was the leader of one of the best defenses in NFL history. For that, he is right in claiming to be one of the best cornerbacks in the league. However, he received a large amount of criticism after that statement because he began to put other players down. He became a reflection of our society, which values the elevation of self above others. How many talented people have you met that have the personality and character of Richard Sherman? Unfortunately, the commonly accepted standard in our culture is to take credit for our accomplishments instead of giving credit where it is due (namely, God).

Balancing talent, hard work, and humility is very difficult. But the following passage helps us keep the right perspective: *Every good gift and every perfect gift is from above, coming down from the Father of lights with whom there is no variation of shadow due to change* (Jas. 1:17, ESV).

We need to remember that "every good gift" comes from God. If that gift is a talent you are blessed with, He wants that talent to be used for His glory.

Keep in mind that we are only stewards of the talents He's given us. Similar to possessions, we cannot take talents with us. Some of the time, talents are only given for a season of life. Therefore, we must not cling too tightly to those talents, but rather we should use them wisely for His kingdom.

We also should not spend the talent just on ourselves or our renown. We should use our gifts and talents to honor God and serve one another. If God has gifted you in sports, then play that sport to the best of your ability. Play hard and give God the credit for your giftedness. Don't put others down on your team; encourage them. If you are an intelligent individual with a promising career, then choose to use your knowledge to help others. Maybe you will find the cure for cancer, or maybe you are a student who could help someone else in your class pass a tough test.

How are you using your talents?

 CONSISTENCY ———

1) A right view of humility. How do you view your talents? Do you view them as something you have earned through hard work, or do you view them as gifts from God? Reflect upon the following passage, and note the humility of Jesus: *Have this mind among yourselves, which is yours in Christ Jesus, who, though he was in the form of God, did not count equality with God a thing to be grasped, but emptied himself, by taking the form of a servant, being born in the likeness of men. And being found in human form, he humbled himself by becoming obedient to the point of death, even death on a cross* (Phil. 2:5-8, ESV).

Jesus chose to give up His rightful divine place to become a man so that you could have a relationship with God. He is the ultimate example of humility.

2) A right view of yourself. When asked about your natural giftedness, do you make much of yourself? Hard work and discipline are great qualities to have. But don't be consumed by the worldly image that you have earned something. Every gift has been given by God and we are called to be good stewards of those gifts. When was the last time you thanked God for your talents?

3) A right view of others. How have you helped others with your talents? Do you strive to help them through your talents and resources, or do you selfishly keep your talents to yourself? God would have been justified if He chose to keep His Son in heaven instead of paying your debt on the cross. Rather, His Word says, *But he was pierced for our transgressions; he was crushed for our iniquities; upon him was the chastisement that brought us peace, and with his wounds we are healed. All we like sheep have gone astray; we have turned—every one—to his own way; and the LORD has laid on him the iniquity of us all* (Isa. 53:5-6, ESV). Jesus chose to sacrifice everything for the benefit of humanity. Are you willing to follow His example?

DAY 6 MECHANICS OF HUMILITY
INTENSITY

Living a life of humility is an ongoing battle for every believer. No matter where you are in your current walk with Christ, it is impossible to completely remove pride. If not careful, pride will rise quickly in our lives and stifle our desire to be thankful for the things God has given us. Following pride's rise comes the sense of entitlement that says we deserve certain things or certain treatment. No matter who you are or what you have accomplished in this lifetime, remember that no one was more entitled than Christ; yet He chose to serve others instead of being served. Mark 10:45 says: *For even the Son of Man did not come to be served, but to serve, and to give his life as a ransom for many* (NIV). The mark of humility is not that you think less of yourself, but that you think of yourself less.

We have spent the last week talking in depth about humility. Now it is time to step up to the plate and apply what we have learned. Remember, knowledge without application produces pride.

Day 1: Accomplishments (Phil. 2:5-7).
1. How did Jesus demonstrate humility? Give examples from Scripture.
2. How do you keep from being prideful in your accomplishments?
3. What steps will you take to turn the attention off of yourself and onto Jesus?

Day 2: Self-Evaluation (Ps. 139:23-24)
1. Are you taking honest assessments of your spiritual life? Explain.
2. How can we help each other in self-evaluation?
3. Why is it important to practice self-evaluation often?

Day 3: Entitlement (Rom. 12:3)

1. To what do you attribute the pervading sense of entitlement in our culture today?
2. How does pride lead to entitlement?
3. Do you battle entitlement in your life? Explain.

Day 4: Gratefulness (1 Thess. 5:18)

1. Do you find the people around you to be grateful or ungrateful? Give an example.
2. Do you find it hard to "give thanks in everything"? Explain.
3. Why is it important to give thanks even in the hard times?

Day 5: Talent (Jas. 1:17)

1. Do you see people using their talents to glorify God or themselves? Explain. How can you use your talents to bring glory to God?
2. How do you maintain a heart of humility?
3. How do you remain confident without being boastful or arrogant?

MECHANICS OF QUALITY VS. QUANTITY

DAY 1 MECHANICS OF QUALITY VS. QUANTITY

BE ACTIVE

But be doers of the word, and not hearers only, deceiving yourselves.
—James 1:22 (ESV)

There are many people in this world who have good intentions, but good intentions without execution produce no results. Today we are focusing on the importance of being proactive. Many people are not satisfied with their current situations (work, fitness, school, spiritual journey, etc.), but very few are making a daily decision to do something about it.

Every January, fitness centers welcome thousands of new members who have New Year resolutions to become more fit. Many of them set goals and make the proper investments in order to find results, but very few of them actually stick to the game plan. How many people have you encountered who had good intentions but failed to endure the long haul?

Spiritual maturity and fitness have much in common. Neither are easy, and both require us to be proactive. Today I challenge you to stop procrastinating and start investing. If you are not invested in studying God's Word, prayer, memorizing Scripture, or being active in your church, then it will be difficult to grow and mature in your faith. Similarly, you don't become physically fit by merely watching people work out. You have to put in the hard work. There is no quick fix to spiritual maturity. No shake weight or diet pill will produce the results you desire. Hard work and daily activity are the keys to maturing as a believer.

In fitness we have a saying, "The goal of fitness is to improve your quality of life and to impact others close to you." Many people spend hours pursuing their fitness goals, but they never put their hard work into application. They will go home and watch TV or surf the Internet for hours without ever utilizing the investment and hard work of being in the gym. The same can happen in our spiritual journey. The goal of being proactive is not to memorize the most Scripture or to attend four different church services on Sunday. Although those are not bad things, the goal of investing in spiritual disciplines is to utilize those resources. For example, one of the reasons we memorize Scripture is to help us resist temptation. Or, one of the reasons to be involved with a local church is to help meet one another's needs and the needs of the community. We must be proactive in seeking God's Word and applying it in our lives. A saying I lived by in college was, "Knowledge without application only results in pride, but how can I ever apply anything I do not know?"

As a member of the CrossFit seminar staff team, my job is to instruct other CrossFitters who desire to become coaches or own a CrossFit gym. In order to be the best CrossFit seminar staff member I can be, I must use my knowledge of CrossFit to teach others how to apply that knowledge in their fitness journeys. I do this by studying anatomy, working out, or coaching a class and bettering other athletes. I must put in the hard work before I ever arrive to our weekend seminar. If not, then I began to look unprofessional or lose my credibility. Part of my job is living out this concept of virtuosity—being the best I can be at the basics and teaching others, who teach others, how to apply those same basic mechanics in their movements. If I know everything there is to know about working out but am a terrible communicator or teacher of those concepts, then I would not be a very effective coach. It is balancing that concept of knowledge and application.

The same balance of knowledge and application holds true in our spiritual journeys. A big part of being proactive in our spiritual maturity is encountering a healthy balance of knowledge and application. As I pursue Christ and grow daily through His Word, I must ask myself the following question: How am I actively applying God's Word today? Spiritual leaders will not only hear God's Word through a daily quiet time, but they will also look for ways to apply God's Word on a daily basis. Spiritual maturity is living a healthy balance of pursuing Christ with spiritual disciplines and applying those disciplines to impact your life and other people's lives.

✵ CONSISTENCY ──────

1) Know and apply God's Word. Remember, "knowledge without application only results in pride, but how can I ever apply anything I do not know?" Try to find a healthy balance of pursuing God's Word and looking for ways to put it into practice.

2) Serve the church. Look for opportunities to invest in your local church. Remember, God is not only looking for hearers of His Word, but He is also looking for those who are living out His Word. I challenge you to become involved in your local church and meet the needs of those around you.

3) Be wise with your time. Do you struggle to have a consistent quiet time? Why? We all have 24 hours in a day. What we value the most will be what we choose to accomplish in those 24 hours.

Look carefully then how you walk, not as unwise but as wise, making the best use of the time, because the days are evil.
—Ephesians 5:15-16 (ESV)

DAY 2: MECHANICS OF QUALITY VS. QUANTITY
MORE IS NOT BETTER, BETTER IS BETTER

For I desire steadfast love and not sacrifice, the knowledge of God rather than burnt offerings. —Hosea 6:6 (ESV)

Hershel Walker said that at the peak of his NFL career he did fifteen hundred push-ups and two thousand sit-ups every single day. He did not have to exercise that way, yet he chose to—not because he wanted to maintain his strength, but because he wanted to get stronger every single day. Spiritually, our lives are no different. If you don't make an effort to grow in your faith, you won't lose your salvation, but your walk with Christ will become stagnant and you will lose your spiritual influence and effectiveness.

We live in a society that rewards the hard worker. Promotions, salary increases, and leadership opportunities often drive people to push themselves to the limits to achieve their goals. Far too many believers take this same approach in their spiritual walk. They think the more they do, the more God will be impressed. Thankfully, the gospel does not work in this manner. God's response to you is not based on your work ethic or your ability to outdo those around you. Jesus has already accomplished all things on the cross, and all He desires in return is obedience.

The question is often asked by a new CrossFitter, "Is more better?" It stands to reason that if you have great results from working out one hour a day, then you should have even better results from working out two, three, or even four hours a day. However, CrossFitters who take this approach often burn themselves out. They fail to realize that there are no shortcuts in fitness. The people who find lasting results are those who are committed for the long haul. They discover that consistency and longevity are key in their Crossfit and fitness journeys. Quality trumps quantity in fitness, and in our spiritual lives as well.

Similar to a new CrossFitter, the natural tendency for a new believer is to believe that more is better—that God loves me because of my performance, so if I do more for Him, He'll love me more. If we allow ourselves to believe this lie, then we nullify what Christ accomplished on the cross. If our spiritual journey was performance based, then Christ's crucifixion on the cross accomplished nothing. Think about it. In believing this lie, we are claiming that our daily performance is of greater worth than Christ's sacrifice. This is a very prideful statement that often causes new believers to fall under a sense of legalism. But remember what God's Word says about our righteous acts: *All of us have become like one who is unclean, and all our righteous acts are like filthy rags* (Isa. 64:6, NIV).

Paul makes it clear that none of us are good unto ourselves: *There is no one righteous, not even one; there is no one who understands; there is no one who seeks God. All have turned away, they have together become worthless; there is no one who does good, not even one* (Rom. 3:10-12, NIV).

So if our righteous acts are not pure in the eyes of Christ, then what is our responsibility as believers? Obedience! God has transformed us, and He requires simple obedience: *I will give them an undivided heart and put a new spirit in them; I will remove from them their heart of stone and give them a heart of flesh. Then they will follow my decrees and be careful to keep my laws. They will be my people, and I will be their God* (Ezek. 11:19-20, NIV).

It really is that simple. Those who have found joy in their walk with Christ have experienced this truth. The quality of Christ's crucifixion trumps the quantity of my performance. More is not better. Yes, God wants you to seek Him with all of your heart: *Call to me and I will answer you and tell you great and unsearchable things you do not know* (Jer. 33:3, NIV). He desires for you to serve Him obediently and faithfully. But please don't fall into the trap that God only loves you based on your daily performance.

So what you are saying is, "just do less"? Not at all. Rather, the goal of today is to communicate that God is more concerned about your heart than your actions: *For I desire steadfast love and not sacrifice, the knowledge of God rather than burnt offerings* (Hos. 6:6, ESV). The goal of every believer is to become more like Christ, not just to do more.

 CONSISTENCY ——————

1) Spend time in God's Word. Take time to read God's Word and memorize it. Don't measure the effectiveness of this discipline by the amount of time you give to it. However, remember that we give time to the things we value. So, don't set a stopwatch on your quiet time, but rest in God's presence and enjoy the time you have with Him. Also, realize that you don't leave His presence when you finish your quiet time. Enjoy His presence throughout the day.

Today, I challenge you to wrestle with God and His Word with no clock and no distractions. Give Him your undivided attention. Say with the psalmist: *One thing have I asked of the LORD, that will I seek after: that I may dwell in the house of the LORD all the days of my life, to gaze upon the beauty of the LORD and to inquire in his temple* (Ps. 27:4, ESV). Strive to be captivated by God's presence today.

2) Remind yourself that your spiritual journey is about growing in your personal relationship with God. It can be tempting to compare your spiritual walk with others', but every one of us is at a different place in our spiritual journeys. God desires one thing. Obedience! Honestly ask yourself, *For am I now seeking the approval of man, or of God? Or am I trying to please man? If I were still trying to please man, I would not be a servant of Christ* (Gal. 1:10, ESV). What is driving your current walk? The approval of man or God? Don't get caught up in what everyone else is doing. Rather, be obedient.

DAY 3 MECHANICS OF QUALITY VS. QUANTITY
LIFE ON PURPOSE

Do you not know that in a race all the runners run, but only one gets the prize? Run in such a way as to get the prize. Everyone who competes in the games goes into strict training. They do it to get a crown that will not last, but we do it to get a crown that will last forever. Therefore I do not run like someone running aimlessly; I do not fight like a boxer beating the air. No, I strike a blow to my body and make it my slave so that after I have preached to others, I myself will not be disqualified for the prize. —1 Corinthians 9:24-27 (NIV)

We have heard the phrase "less is more." A short, intense workout has been proven to have more impact than a longer, less-intense workout. It goes back to the basics of physics (Power = [force x distance]/time). The goal of CrossFit is to increase work capacity across broad time and modal domains. That is a fancy way of saying doing more work in less time. You do not have to work out for hours a day to find results. Rather, a short, intense workout session will produce better results.

Consdier the person who walks on the treadmill for hours every day. There is nothing wrong with a person walking on a treadmill or around a track. However, without ever increasing their pace or changing their workout, their body will become accustomed to what they are doing, and they will fail to produce the results they are looking to achieve. Again, it goes back to physics (Power = [force x distance]/time). Think of power being our results. From physics class we know that force times distance is equal to work. Therefore, we believe that results equal the hard work you put in. If you are doing the same routine over and over again, then you are going to get the same results. There are many believers who take this same approach in their faith.

As Christians we might determine that if we attend more church services, read the Bible more, spend long hours in prayer, listen to lots of Christian music, hang with the "right" people, date church girls, and so on, then these things will make us Christians or better Christians. This describes a faith that is built around quantity, also known as a works-based faith. This is a faith built around the Devil's lies, which is no faith at all.

We as men need a clear understanding that our faith is more about quality than quantity. Paul says it this way in 1 Corinthians 9:24-27: *Do you not know that in a race all the runners run, but only one gets the prize? Run in such a way as to get the prize. Everyone who competes in the games goes into strict training. They do it to get a crown that will not last, but we do it to get a crown that will last forever. Therefore I do not run like someone running aimlessly; I do not fight like a boxer beating the air. No, I strike a blow to my body and make it my slave so that after I have preached to others, I myself will not be disqualified for the prize* (NIV).

We as young men should *run in such a way as to get the prize.* The runner who is running to win wants to win! He is not running just because that is what he's supposed to do. The guys who do that are finishing in last place. Followers of Christ should be striving for excellence in their walk with Christ, therefore they do what is right because they want to, not because they feel obligated. A works-based faith says, "We should change the music we listen to, the language we use, the girls we date, the images we look at, and so on simply because that is what we must do to belong to Christ and not the world." When you live a life on purpose, however, you're waking up each day with a passion in your heart to live that day for Christ! The question you have to ask yourself is: Am I running through life with a cause and purpose or am I running through life aimlessly? Only you can answer that for yourself. I challenge you to pause and do a self-evaluation right now. Remember, if you aim at nothing, you'll hit it every time. You will never be able to fight off the schemes of the enemy—which is the Devil—if you don't wake up each day aiming for the things of Christ.

CONSISTENCY ———

1. Memorize Scripture with a purpose. Instead of trying to memorize 365 verses this year, what if you committed to memorize 12 verses, one a month. Choose 12 that could have great impact on your life. Here are 12 verses to consider this year:

> Exodus 2:20—Remembering the Sabbath
> Job 31:1—Struggling with lust
> Psalm 27:14—Waiting on the Lord
> Psalm 37:7—Be still
> Isaiah 43:1—Fear not
> Luke 6:46—Obedience
> Luke 9:23—Surrender
> John 3:16—Salvation
> I Corinthians 16:13—Stand firm
> Ephesians 2:8—God's grace
> Ephesians 6:10-20—Put on the armor of God
> Philippians 4:13—I can do all things through Christ

2. Spend time in God's Word daily with purpose. Many guys struggle to read more than five minutes in a day. However, good leaders are usually good readers. So spiritual leaders need to be reading the Word of God. Instead of picking a long reading plan, pick one with purpose for your life. Here are two I recommend to you:

> - Checkpoints: A Tactical Guide to Manhood by Brian Mills and Nathan Wagnon
> - The Joshua Code by O. S. Hawkins

3. Self-Evaluate. Constantly evaluate your walk with Christ. Take a few minutes to list in your journal, or maybe in the notes page on your phone, four disciplines that are making you stronger in your walk with Christ. Reading this book can be one of them. Remember it is not how much you do, but what you do and how you do it that matters most.

DAY 4: MECHANICS OF QUALITY VS. QUANTITY
INTENTIONAL LIVING

I have been crucified with Christ and I no longer live, but Christ lives in me. The life I now live in the body, I live by faith in the Son of God, who loved me and gave himself for me. —Galatians 2:20 (NIV)

Intentional living is rare among guys today. We lose intentionality when we focus more on what we can get out of something than what we can give to it. Intentional men think *What can I provide for this team?* Selfish men think *What can this team provide for me?* We have to move from a getting to a giving attitude if we are going to become men of intentionality.

We see this all the time on *ESPN* or the *SEC network* (yes, I love that channel) where college-bound athletes pick a team simply to see what that team can do for them. This does not just happen in sports, though. How many big bands will play on a smaller stage once they "make it"? The stage becomes more about what it can do for them.

To get physically stronger you have to push yourself to give more if you ever want to achieve the body you've dreamed of. To be the best musician you have to push yourself and "give up so you can go up." In all things you have to be intentional if you want to be the best. We have to take the stage that has been placed in front of us and be intentional with every moment.

When a guy walks into the locker room for the first time, he may walk in with some insecurities and a strong desire to be accepted. He will then do what is needed to get acceptance. What if that same guy walked into the locker room thinking, How can I give to this team so that I can earn their favor? Once favor is earned, influenced is earned, and when you earn influence, the reward is leadership. Leaders never rise to the top by being like everyone else, doing the same work as everyone else, or even getting everyone to accept them. Leaders rise to the top by being intentional with their lives. Intentional living is uncommon. We need more uncommon men today who live their lives on purpose.

Paul wanted it to be known that he was not under the law but a committed follower of Christ. He intentionally allowed God to work through him so that he could make much of Christ with his life. I love how John McArthur puts it: "The true Christian life is not so much a believer living for Christ as Christ's living though the believer."[7] Paul was put under house arrest soon after writing to the Galatians. There he penned a letter to the Philippians where he again addressed his intentionality toward the way he lived his life: *I eagerly expect and hope that I will in no way be ashamed, but will have sufficient courage so that now as always Christ will be exalted in my body, whether by life or by death. For to me, to live is Christ and to die is gain* (Phil. 1:20-21, NIV).

We need intentional men today who are willing to choose Christ no matter what. God has placed you on that team, in that locker room, in that club, at that place of employment, in that band, or wherever. God has placed you in that environment to live intentionally so He may be made famous through you.

 CONSISTENCY ———

1. Live Intentionally. Recognize that God has a purpose for placing you in your environment. God has given you certain talents and gifts. He wants you to use those talents and gifts intentionally to bring Him glory.

2. Serve Intentionally. If you are not living intentionally you will miss those that God has placed in your life on purpose. You may miss it simply because you are more focused on what you can get out of this relationship instead of what you can give to it. Don't miss out on how God wants to use you to serve the people who come into your life.

3. Walk Intentionally. Where are you walking or going today? Are you going with intentional purpose or are you just going? Most guys would say, "I've never thought about it; I guess I am just going." Change that mindset today from "I am just going," to "God, use me as I go to bring glory to You."

DAY 5: MECHANICS OF QUALITY VS. QUANTITY
PUTTING IN THE REPS

I have fought the good fight, I have finished the race, and I have kept the faith. —2 Timothy 4:7 (NIV)

Nothing in this life comes easy. Achieving your goals requires persistence and discipline. If you want something, you must be willing to make sacrifices. When Muhammad Ali was asked how many sit-ups he did in a day, he responded, "I don't count my sit-ups. I only start counting when it starts hurting. That is when I start counting, because then it really counts. That's what makes you a champion."[8] No one ever became the greatest at their profession by coincidence. All great champions chose to put in the extra reps. What if Christians chose to take this same approach in seeking to know God and His will?

Many want to be used by God, but few are willing to put in the hard work. God is building champions, godly young men to accomplish His plans. Look at the young man David when he killed Goliath in battle. His victory didn't happen by chance. Rather, he had been in training. The Bible speaks of David killing both a lion and a bear while protecting his sheep before his encounter with Goliath: *David answered Saul: "Your servant has been tending his father's sheep. Whenever a lion or a bear came and carried off a lamb from the flock, I went after it, struck it down, and rescued the lamb from its mouth. If it reared up against me, I would grab it by its fur, strike it down, and kill it. Your servant has killed lions and bears; this uncircumcised Philistine will be like one of them, for he has defied the armies of the living God." Then David said, "The LORD who rescued me from the paw of the lion and the paw of the bear will rescue me from the hand of this Philistine." Saul said to David, "Go, and may the LORD be with you"* (1 Sam. 17:34-37).

David was far from a passive man and had been preparing himself for battle long before his encounter with Goliath. His preparation had included both protecting his sheep and being led by God's Spirit (1 Sam. 16:13). God desires to use men today as He did David. Unfortunately, there are very few men who are preparing themselves to be used by God like David.

If you want to become a champion and be used by God, you must train yourself in the following areas.

1) Put in the reps of seeking to know God and His will. The best way of seeking God and His will comes from spending time in His Word: *All Scripture is God-breathed and is useful for teaching, rebuking, correcting and training in righteousness, so that the man of God may be thoroughly equipped for every good work* (2 Tim. 3:16-17, NIV). There is no easy journey. Only those who are truly committed will endure through the long haul.

2) Train yourself to be faithful where God currently has you. He has placed you there for His purpose: *For we are his workmanship, created in Christ Jesus for good works, which God prepared beforehand, that we should walk in them* (Eph. 2:10, ESV). Are you making the most of your opportunities? David was a faithful shepherd before he was God's chosen king. God has a purpose and vision for every one of our lives. He requires one thing—obedience. May we walk in the path that He has chosen for our lives.

To become a champion requires disciplined hard work. There is no shortcut. The same holds true for God's champions. They are persistent in seeking to know God and choosing to live in obedience to His will. They never waver through the storms of life, but strive to become more like Christ. God's champions don't make excuses ("It's too early," "I have had a long day," or "I don't have time"). Instead, they choose to daily invest in God's Word and seek to be used by Him in the present and the future. God's champions (similar to David) are not built overnight. They make sacrifices; they are resilient; they endure. If you desire to be used by God, then ask yourself: How am I currently investing?

✴ CONSISTENCY ———

1. Are you being faithful in making daily investments in God's Word? (2 Tim. 3:16-17)

2. Are you being faithful in storing God's Word into your heart? *I have stored up your word in my heart, that I might not sin against you* (Ps. 119:11, ESV).

3. Are you being faithful where God currently has you? It is very difficult to become a great leader if you are not currently being faithful with what God has given you. We are all called to be good stewards of the gifts God has given us.

Some may have been given more than others, but the calling is still the same. Obedience. Live this verse: *Whatever you do, work heartily, as for the Lord and not for men, knowing that from the Lord you will receive the inheritance as your reward. You are serving the Lord Christ* (Col. 3:23-24, ESV).

4. Stop making excuses and put in the reps! It can become easy to make excuses and not put in quality reps. There are many people who have good intentions. Good intentions without application will produce no results. No one ever became fit overnight. Rather, it is a daily decision to wake up and put in quality reps. The same holds true for our spiritual fitness. It is impossible to grow and mature as a believer unless we are willing to put in quality time to know God. Set a specific time to meet with God this week and stick with it. We do this every day with our work, workouts, or dates. Why should our time with God be any different?

Look carefully then how you walk, not as unwise but as wise, making the best use of the time, because the days are evil. —**Ephesians 5:15-16 (ESV).**

DAY 6 MECHANICS OF QUALITY VS. QUANTITY

INTENSITY

More is not always better. The quantity concept drives our current society (work 40 hours a week, work out for 90 minutes a day, or go to school for 8 hours a day), but it fails to answer a simple question: how does it take exactly 40 hours a week to complete my work, or 8 hours a day to do school work, or exactly 90 minutes to produce the fitness results I am looking for? That answer is very simple. It doesn't, and it has been proved otherwise by business owners, homeschoolers, and CrossFitters. More is not better. Better is better. Quality, not quantity, produces the results we are looking for, and our spiritual journey is no different.

This concept of a quantity-based system can affect our spiritual journeys. Spiritual disciplines were designed to help us grow closer to Christ, not as an end in themselves. The goal is not to memorize more Scripture than everyone else, or to read a thousand Christian books, or have a four-hour quiet time. Instead, God is more concerned about your intimacy. Honestly assess if you are becoming more intimate with God or not. As believers, we should focus more on the quality of our spiritual walk instead of simply doing more. After all, Christ has already accomplished everything on the cross: *For all have sinned and fall short of the glory of God, and are justified by his grace as a gift, through the redemption that is in Christ Jesus, whom God put forward as a propitiation by his blood, to be received by faith. This was to show God's righteousness, because in his divine forbearance he had passed over former sins. It was to show his righteousness at the present time, so that he might be just and the justifier of the one who has faith in Jesus* (Rom. 3:23-26, ESV).

Ultimately Christianity is not about us; it is about Christ.

Day 1: Be Active – James 1:22

1. On Day 1 you read "good intentions without execution produces no results." How do you get results out of your intentions?
2. How are you actively applying God's Word daily in your life?
3. How do you accept the challenge to "stop doing and start becoming who God intended you to be"?

Day 2: More Is Not Better, Better Is Better – Hosea 6:6

1. The society we live in today rewards hard work. How does that motivate your inner drive?
2. How do you reject a works-based faith and run to a grace-filled faith?
3. How do you find yourself being captivated by God's grace daily?

Day 3: Life on Purpose – 1 Corinthians 9:24-27

1. If you had two weeks to live, how would that change your life? Read Psalm 90:12, and discover how numbering your days would impact the way you live your life.
2. What wrong priority hinders your complete devotion to God?
3. Do you wake up daily and aim for the things of Christ? Explain.

Day 4: Intentional Living – Galatians 2:20

1. What steps can you take to know Jesus in a more intimate way?
2. Matthew 6:33 says, *Seek first the kingdom of God* (ESV). What steps do you need to take to live intentionally before God?
3. If you know God, you love God; if you love God, you trust God. Do you see yourself fully trusting God today? If not, why not?

Day 5: Putting in the Reps – 2 Timothy 4:7

1. Read 1 Corinthians 9:25-27. In your personal pursuit of Jesus, are you running "aimlessly" or "beating the air"? Explain.
2. What does your spiritual training look like?
3. What does a lifestyle of faithfulness look like daily?

MECHANICS OF DISCIPLINE

DAY 1 MECHANICS OF DISCIPLINE
ONE DAY AT A TIME

And he said to all, "If anyone would come after me, let him deny himself and take up his cross daily and follow me." —Luke 9:23 (ESV)

"Every day that we're not practicing godliness we're being conformed to the world of ungodliness around us."[9] –Jerry Bridges, *The Fruitful Life*

Jerry Bridges explains in his books *The Fruitful Life* and *The Discipline of Grace* that we are all growing into either Christlikeness or worldliness. There is no in-between. If you struggle with that concept, then think in terms of your fitness. You are either becoming more fit every day by the decisions you make (exercise and eating habits) or your fitness is decreasing.

CrossFit CEO Greg Glassman has an idea of a fitness, wellness, and sickness continual. His argument is that people are either becoming more fit or unfit by their daily decisions. This concept can also hold true for our spiritual fitness. We are either becoming more fit or unfit based on our daily spiritual decisions. No one ever dropped off the deep end overnight. Rather, it was a daily decision to follow their flesh rather than the spirit. Our flesh and spirit are in constant tension with one another: *But I say, walk by the Spirit, and you will not gratify the desires of the flesh. For the desires of the flesh are against the Spirit, and the desires of the Spirit are against the flesh, for these are opposed to each other, to keep you from doing the things you want to do* (Gal. 5:16-17, ESV).

How do you fight off the flesh and pursue spiritual fitness? It starts through healthy spiritual decisions. Every morning we have a choice— to pursue God and His Word or pursue the ways of this world. When we make healthy spiritual decisions (pursuing God's Word, accountability, prayer, and other spiritual disciplines), we grow in spiritual maturity and become fit to take on the work of God. Every person who is fit (spiritually or physically) had to work hard for it.

Many people are captivated by athletic champions (i.e. Michael Jordan, Michael Phelps, Tiger Woods), and they wonder how they too can become the best in their sport. The answer is hard work on a daily basis. Each champion put in the work and chose to better themselves every day. The same holds true for the spiritual giants of our past decades (John Calvin, Jonathan Edwards, John Piper). They too chose to seek God on a consistent and daily basis and be faithful to Him. If we desire the same outcome, then we must willfully choose to take up our crosses daily and follow Christ.

The journey to spiritual fitness requires both discipline and sacrifice. It requires you to put on Christlikeness and to put off the things of this world: *You were taught, with regard to your former way of life, to put off your old self, which is being corrupted by its deceitful desires; to be made new in the attitude of your minds; and to put on the new self, created to be like God in true righteousness and holiness* (Eph. 4:22-24, NIV). In order to be spiritually mature, we must both train ourselves in righteousness and flee from sinfulness. If we do one without the other, then we will not find the results we are seeking. It would be the same as working out every day, and then eating unhealthy for every meal. If we want to mature spiritually, we must be disciplined (training in righteousness) and make sacrifices (flee from sinfulness).

Jesus calls us to pick up our crosses daily and follow Him (Luke 9:23). What does that mean? Christian living requires dying to the world. The cross represented the worst punishable death of Jesus' time. It was designed to publicly humiliate a person and make them suffer unto death. Jesus knew exactly what He was saying when He challenged His disciples to pick up their crosses and follow Him. He was challenging them to die to themselves and choose humility. He knew their journey would not be easy. He knew the disciples would have to sacrifice everything in order to follow Him. The same still holds true. If you desire to follow Christ, you must first pick up your cross. Intentionally choose to live for Christ and die to this world. This is no easy task, and those who do it are few: *Enter through the narrow gate. For wide is the gate and broad is the road that leads to destruction, and many enter through it. But small is the gate and narrow the road that leads to life, and only a few find it* (Matt. 7:13-14, NIV).

The key word is *daily*. Those who mature as believers intentionally spend quality time in God's Word and prayer. They are disciplined in their faith and hold fast to God's promises. They cling to God's Word and choose to pick up their crosses daily. Though it may be inconvenient, keep the sacrifice of Jesus in mind. He counted it joy to endure the cross that we might become co-heirs in God's kingdom: *Looking to Jesus, the founder and perfecter of our faith, who for the joy that was set before him endured the cross, despising the shame, and is seated at the right hand of the throne of God* (Heb. 12:2, ESV).

May we too find it a daily joy to spend time in God's Word and know the Author and Perfecter of our faith.

⊗ CONSISTENCY ———

1) Do you find it a joy or burden to spend time in God's Word? Can you relate with the psalmist when he says, *As a deer pants for flowing streams, so pants my soul for you, O God. My soul thirsts for God, for the living God. When shall I come and appear before God?* (Ps. 42:1-2, ESV). Strive to find joy in spending time daily in God's Word.

2) How spiritually fit are you? Remember that growing as a believer requires two parts: putting on righteousness and putting off worldliness: *To put off your old self, which belongs to your former manner of life and is corrupt through deceitful desires, and to be renewed in the spirit of your minds, and to put on the new self, created after the likeness of God in true righteousness and holiness* (Eph. 4:22-24, ESV). Identify the one you struggle with the most and form accountability to help you become spiritually fit.

DAY 2 MECHANICS OF DISCIPLINE

COUNT THE COST

I will follow you wherever you go. —Luke 9:57 (ESV)

To achieve anything of significance in life, we must first be willing to count the cost. Many people say they want to be the best at something, but very few are willing to sacrifice. On his road to being the greatest Olympian of all time, Michael Phelps trained six days a week for five or six hours a day. His journey to winning 18 gold medals was not an accident. Instead, it was achieved by intentional planning the appropriate sacrifices. It was reported that Phelps would swim a minimum of 80,000 meters a week. That is an equivalent of 50 miles! In order to do so, he had to make sacrifices with his family, friends, and anything else that keep him from achieving his goal.[10]

It's hard to make sacrifices without a vision or goal. Great athletes are able to make sacrifices because they know what they want. Whether it is a desire to be the best on the team or win a championship, everyone has to know why they are sacrificing. The journey to the top does not happen by chance. It requires being disciplined and making the appropriate sacrifices. It is very inconvenient, so you must first count the cost.

Counting the cost is simply evaluating the risk versus the reward. The greater the goal, the more you have to be willing to risk. Every person naturally does this, but very few actually evaluate the pros and cons. People often sacrifice family or friends to be great athletes or having successful careers. The question they must ask themselves is, *Is it really worth it?* Is that next promotion or winning the championship really worth the sacrifice? Each person has to answer for himself.

Paul provided an illustration of the similarities of an athlete and a Christian, and how both require discipline and sacrifice: *Do you not know that in a race all the runners run, but only one receives the prize?*

So run that you may obtain it. Every athlete exercises self-control in all things. They do it to receive a perishable wreath, but we an imperishable. So I do not run aimlessly; I do not box as one beating the air. But I discipline my body and keep it under control, lest after preaching to others I myself should be disqualified (1 Cor. 9:24-27, ESV).

Paul knew exactly who he was playing for and the sacrifices he was willing to take. He knew that there were great athletes who made sacrifices to achieve great things, but those things were temporary. Paul, however, was willing to risk all for the reward of knowing Christ and making His name known. He says in Philippians: *But whatever gain I had, I counted as loss for the sake of Christ. Indeed, I count everything as loss because of the surpassing worth of knowing Christ Jesus my Lord. For his sake I have suffered the loss of all things and count them as rubbish, in order that I may gain Christ* (Phil. 3:7-8, ESV). For Paul, the choice was simple. He was willing to sacrifice all for the sake of Christ.

We all have goals in life and aspire to do great things. However, we must ask ourselves if the risk is worth the reward. If we are willing to sacrifice, then the reward must be great. The goal of Christianity is not to spend eternity in heaven. Instead, the goal is to make Jesus' name known. Heaven just comes as a by-product of our desire to be with God. There is no greater reward than the opportunity to spend eternity with our Savior. Regardless of the hardships, persecutions, or sacrifices we may face in this lifetime, the reward is far greater than the risk! The choice is ultimately yours. What kind of legacy are you going to leave? And what are you willing to sacrifice to leave it?

✺ CONSISTENCY ───

1) Make a list. List the top three things you desire to achieve in this lifetime, and ask yourself what you are willing to risk in order to accomplish those things.

Goals are great things to have in life, and every one of us should have goals for different aspects of our lives. But remember that every goal requires some level of sacrifice. Look back at your list and note the things you're not willing to sacrifice to achieve your goals.

For example, maybe you would like to play a collegiate sport one day, but you are not willing to practice Wednesday night because you do not want to miss Bible study.

2) What am I willing to risk to make Jesus' name known? Commit to memory the following passage if you struggle with making Jesus' name known around your family or friends: *But whatever gain I had, I counted as loss for the sake of Christ. Indeed, I count everything as loss because of the surpassing worth of knowing Christ Jesus my Lord. For his sake I have suffered the loss of all things and count them as rubbish, in order that I may gain Christ* (Phil. 3:7-8, ESV).

There is no greater goal we can have in this lifetime than to make Jesus' name known. The reward far outweighs the risk! God's Word says: *For a day in your courts is better than a thousand elsewhere. I would rather be a doorkeeper in the house of my God than dwell in the tents of wickedness* (Ps. 84:10, ESV). Nothing in this lifetime will ever compare to the joy and love God desires to share with those who are faithful to His calling.

DAY 3 MECHANICS OF DISCIPLINE
COMPLACENCY

Not that I have already obtained all this, or have already arrived at my goal, but I press on to take hold of that for which Christ Jesus took hold of me. Brothers and sisters, I do not consider myself yet to have taken hold of it. But one thing I do: Forgetting what is behind and straining toward what is ahead, I press on toward the goal to win the prize for which God has called me heavenward in Christ Jesus.
—Philippians 3:12-14 (NIV)

You will often hear athletes admit to becoming complacent after failed or poor results, but certainly not before. It was not until they lost, or simply underperformed, that they came to realize they let their guard down. Margaux Alvarez has been competing in the CrossFit Games and has always longed to win. The thing that held her back in 2013 was her gymnastics movements. She then made this statement: "We can't just be complacent. We have to be ready. We have to drill those movements—the handstand push-ups, handstand walks or muscle-ups—and yet continue to build upon my strengths."[11]

Alvarez could have said that her gymnastics movements are good enough and she just needs to be in better shape. But she knew that she couldn't be complacent if she wanted to win. She had to improve on doing the common parts of the games uncommonly well.

Have you ever experienced a time in your life when you got out of a routine and began to experience the consequences of being complacent? Maybe you woke up and looked in the mirror and realized that you were unsatisfied with your current situation. You didn't get there overnight. Instead, it came as a by-product of complacency. This same type of complacency can filter into our spiritual lives.

I believe this happens constantly to guys. You know God is calling you, and at times you have really picked it up in your walk with Christ.

You begin to live a holier life. Then your commitment starts to fade and before you know it you say, "Oh well," and you give up. In that moment, you have become indifferent about your walk with Christ. All discipline goes out the window and you live a carefree life because, "you just don't care."

Complacency is the same as the sin of indifference. The sin of indifference is when you stop caring and surrender to the things of the world. Guys all over the world today are struggling with the sin of indifference. We give up on the command to stay sexually pure until marriage for that one lustful moment. We give up on a meaningful relationship because we don't feel it is worth the fight. We give up on that sport because our coach is riding us too hard. We give up on our leadership because we want to be accepted by the crowd. We give up because our complacent heart stops listening to the voice of God in our lives. As a result, we start listening to all the voices of this world.

Because the sin of indifference has crept into our lives, we miss opportunities to leave legacies. We miss opportunities to reach friends. We miss opportunities to impact the lives of others.

Paul says in Philippians 3:12, *Not that I have already obtained this or am already perfect, but I press on to make it my own, because Christ Jesus has made me his own* (ESV).

Paul is referring to what he wrote in verses 1-11 on the challenge to remain righteous. We need to stop here and be challenged to make our faith in Christ our own. When we own our faith, we stick with it and remain faithful to it. Own your faith in Christ. After all, it is you who made the decision to accept God's salvation call; so own it!

Philippians 3:13 states: *Brothers, I do not consider that I have made it my own* (ESV). Paul shared that it was a challenge for him to live this out, but he did not quit: *But one thing I do: forgetting what lies behind and straining forward to what lies ahead*.

I encourage you today to forget about the past and the mistakes that keep pushing you to live a complacent life. Look forward to what God wants you to be.

Paul continued to challenge us in verse 14, which states, *I press on toward the goal for the prize of the upward call of God in Christ Jesus* (ESV).

Men who become disciplined followers of Christ press on!

⊗ CONSISTENCY ———

1. Check your complacency. Where have you become complacent in your walk with Christ? You cannot change what you do not recognize. At times, you will stumble and fall. That does not mean you should give up and stop fighting the fight God has called you to. In your life, where have you stopped fighting and caved to the sin of indifference?

2. Write out a spiritual mission statement for yourself. The Bible teaches us that where there is no vision, the people parish. (See Prov. 29:18.) Do you have direction for your walk with Christ? What is your mission? Author Brian Mills has taken his last name and made it his family's mission statement. M – Memories, I – Integrity, L – Love, L – Leadership, and S – Salvation. A spiritual mission statement will lead you away from a complacent lifestyle.

3. Surround yourself with great people. I was once told that in order to be an "A" person, you must hang closely to "A" people. If you want to stay focused and not get a "whatever" attitude toward Christ, you must walk alongside others who have those same desires. Who you surround yourself with matters. Think through who your closest friends are, and then evaluate if they are pushing you toward your spiritual mission statement.

DAY 4 MECHANICS OF DISCIPLINE
SET HIGH STANDARDS

You shall be holy, for I am holy. —1 Peter 1:16 (ESV)

As believers, we are called to a standard. Our standard is Christlikeness. That means that every day we strive to be transformed into the image of Christ: *And we all, with unveiled face, beholding the glory of the Lord, are being transformed into the same image from one degree of glory to another. For this comes from the Lord who is the Spirit* (2 Cor. 3:18, ESV). If Christ is not our standard, then it will become easy to settle for less than what God intended for us.

How many talented athletes have you met who did not reach their full potential due to complacency? As a college strength and conditioning coach, I met a wide range of athletes. Some were extremely talented, and others were extremely driven. But very few were both talented and driven. For those gifted athletes, they usually had their minds set on a higher standard. Many of the college athletes were content with playing sports at a collegiate level, but a select few had their eyes set on the NFL, NBA, or MLB. They were the difference makers on the team. You could see it in the way they practiced, lifted weights, and presented themselves on game day. Never settling with one less rep, but always choosing to live out the standard for themselves and their teammates.

God has called us to this same standard in our spiritual walk. The apostle Paul says, *Rather train yourself for godliness; for while bodily training is of some value, godliness is of value in every way, as it holds promise for the present life and also for the life to come* (1 Tim. 4:7-8, ESV). What if believers took that same athletic mentality and applied it to their faith? What if they pictured Jesus as the Captain of the team and strived to follow His example? That is what Paul did. He challenged others by saying, *Be imitators of me, as I am of Christ*

(1 Cor. 11:1, ESV). Paul knew to fix his eyes on Christ. He knew that the only way he could lead other men was by pursuing Christlikeness. Paul was never content with being "good" by a worldly standard. Rather, he trained himself to be more like Christ every day. Did he ever achieve perfection? No, but he "pressed on" every day, knowing that he would only be perfected at the end of his journey when he would ascend to heaven. The same should hold true for us in our journey. Are we perfect? Not even close, but we should strive (like Paul) to be more like Christ every day: *Not that I have already obtained this or am already perfect, but I press on to make it my own, because Christ Jesus has made me his own* (Phil. 3:12, ESV).

Complacency prevents a believer from knowing God more intimately. In our spiritual journey, we should never be content with our current understanding of God. Nor should there be a moment that we think we have everything figured out. A growing believer is also a humble believer. He or she is dependent upon God and seeks to live out His will through knowing His Word. The moment we become complacent in our understanding of God is the same moment we begin to lose our impact for His kingdom. Think of it in this way: What happens when an athlete begins to think that they can have the same level of success apart from their coach? The athlete fails to realize that it was only through the coach's guidance and direction that the team was successful. The same prideful mentality corrupts believers. Some believers begin to think that they could do things on there own apart from God's daily guidance (the Bible). Similar to the athlete, the believer fails to realize that it was only through God's Word and what Christ has accomplished that there was success in the first place. No amount of talent will prevail apart from God's Word. It doesn't matter if you are the most successful, best-looking, most talented person on the earth. You will not succeed unless you have a daily reliance of God's Word in your life. The standard will always be Christlikeness, and maintaining that standard requires intimacy with God through a daily relationship with Him.

 CONSISTENCY ———

1) Who are you currently striving to be like? If the answer is not Christ, then ask yourself why. Christ is the standard for all believers: *You therefore must be perfect, as your heavenly Father is perfect* (Matt. 5:48, ESV). Do not be intimidated by Jesus' command. You will never be perfect in this life, but you can rest assured that Jesus' perfection is sufficient for all your shortcomings. As Paul said, *For our sake he made him to be sin who knew no sin, so that in him we might become the righteousness of God* (2 Cor. 5:21, ESV). You have been made holy in Christ. Not only did He take your sin, He gave you His righteousness.

Your response should be loving obedience as you seek to be more like Christ every day. And you can rest assured that *He who started a good work in you will carry it on to completion until the day of Christ Jesus* (Phil. 1:6). One day all of your shortcomings and imperfections will be perfected when you meet God in heaven.

2) Strive to know God more every day. As a believer, you should never be content in your current understanding of God. His ways are profound and beyond human comprehension: *Oh, the depth of the riches both of the wisdom and the knowledge of God! How unsearchable His judgments and untraceable His ways! For who has known the mind of the Lord? Or who has been His counselor?* (Rom. 11:33-34)

DAY 5 MECHANICS OF DISCIPLINE
COMMITMENT

"You do not want to leave too, do you?" Jesus asked the Twelve.
—John 6:67 (NIV)

"It is not the critic who counts, not the man who points out how the strong man stumbled or where the doer of deeds could have done better. The credit belongs to the man who is actually in the arena; whose face is marred by dust and sweat and blood; who strives valiantly; who errs and comes short again and again; who knows the great enthusiasms, the great devotion, and spends himself in a worthy cause; who, at the best, knows in the end the triumph of high achievement; and who, at the worst, if he fails, at least fails while daring greatly, so that his place shall never be with those cold and timid souls who know neither victory nor defeat."[12] –Theodore Roosevelt

Discipline requires commitment, and commitment requires discipline. These two words build upon one another and seem to be forgotten in our current society. Too many marriages are ending in divorce. Commitment and respect between parents and their teenagers seems to be on a continual decline. I have watched many young men start a sport or an activity and quit halfway through because they did not get what they wanted. Today's culture has a great lack of discipline and commitment. This deficit leads to compromise in our character.

As followers of Christ, we are called to be fully committed to Him in a culture that lacks commitment. Yet in some ways we have developed a spineless generation of Christ followers. When times get hard, insults come, and disagreements happen, we cave and follow the way of the world instead of the way of Christ.

Even the disciples found Jesus' ways to be challenging. In John 6 Jesus performed two miracles. First, He fed the 5,000 with five loaves and two fish. Then, He walked on water and calmed the storm.

He arrived on the other side of the lake and gave a strong challenge of commitment to His followers. While speaking in the synagogue in Capernaum, He proclaimed to be the Bread of life and stated that to follow Him one must eat His flesh and drink His blood. In verse 60 His followers looked at Him and said, *This is a hard teaching* (NIV). *Who can accept it?* Then in verse 66 it says, *From this time many of his disciples turned back and no longer followed him*.

When called to follow with complete devotion and commitment, many walk away. Strength does not come on the mountaintop; it comes on the journey to the mountaintop. If you quit halfway you will never experience the full blessings that are ahead. Ask the extreme hiker who never made it to the top of the mountain. He would tell you, "I wish I would have finished no matter how tired I became." So many give up and quit when they are so close to the top.

Walking with Christ is a journey and requires great discipline. We need godly young men to say that no matter what is thrown at them, what conditions they have to face, or what persecution they may encounter, they will follow Jesus.

May we never quit or give up on the One who never has given up on us. May we say at the end of our lives that we were fully devoted followers of Christ who gave it our all.

⊗ CONSISTENCY ———

1. We all face hard times. How are the hard times affecting you? Every Christian is going to experience difficulty. In those moments you need to trust God's purpose, persevere and stay committed to Christ's work in and through your life. In what area of your life are you wavering on your commitment to Christ?

2. Confess. Confession means agreeing with God about your sin. The Greek word in 1 John 1:9 for "confess" is *homologue*, which simply means "to say the same thing" and then "agree, admit, acknowledge."

Our sin has been forgiven but we must confess it to God. In O.S. Hawkins' book *The Joshua Code*, he says, "Sin is not some little vice that we can laugh off. Sin is so serious that it necessitated the cross."[13] What sin do you need to confess today that is causing your lack of commitment to Christ?

3. Change! If you stay where you are, you will never grow or develop to become what God intends you to be. The ones in the CrossFit gym who don't want to get better or stronger never do. They lack commitment. The same is true in a spiritual journey. If you're not committed to grow and mature in your walk with Christ, you will not. So what do you need to do? Change! Commit today to be a fully devoted follower of Christ, then follow it up with action.

DAY 6 MECHANICS OF DISCIPLINE

INTENSITY

Growing and maturing as a believer requires discipline and perseverance. Spiritual maturity does not happen by chance. Instead, it is an intentional daily decision to become more like Jesus. Discipline is easy to some, but very difficult for many. It's easy to do the things we enjoy, but extremely difficult to do the things that seem like a burden. This becomes a foundational issue for many believers. Instead of viewing spending time with God as a joy, many view it as a burden. This kind of mindset produces a weak level of commitment to God and other believers. Being disciplined is the key to spiritual fitness and allows us to fight the battle of complacency. No one ever achieved anything of significance by being lazy. God has called each and every one of us to be good stewards of the time and resources He has given us: *Look carefully then how you walk, not as unwise but as wise, making the best use of the time, because the days are evil* (Eph. 5:15-16, ESV). In order to be good stewards, we must fight the temptation to become lazy or stagnant in our walk. We must examine our lives and schedules as believers and seek to make the most of every opportunity. Discipline allows us to become the men God has called us to be. We no longer make excuses about why we cannot do things. Instead, we clothe ourselves with a new spirit that drives our training in righteousness. As believers, we must choose to make decisions that put us in a position to be used by God. Many want to be spiritual leaders, but very few are willing to be disciplined and put in the necessary work to become leaders. Champions are not made the day they win something; they are made during countless hours of training. God's leaders are no different.

Day 1: One Day at a Time – Luke 9:23

1. What are three decisions that you can make daily to increase your spiritual health?
2. Do you find it hard to be spiritually fit? Explain.
3. How can you fight the flesh in seeking to stay spiritually fit?

Day 2: Count the Cost – Luke 9:57

1. What does it cost you to follow Christ?
2. Are the risks worth the rewards? Explain.
3. Who can hold you accountable to staying focused on your spiritual goals?

Day 3: Complacency – Philippians 3:12-14

1. Have you ever been complacent in your life? Explain.
2. You were challenged to press on in Philippians. When you read this challenge, does it motivate or discourage you? Explain.
3. What do you think leads to complacency? What needs to change for you to move out of complacency

Day 4: Set High Standards – 1 Peter 1:16

1. What does it mean to be Christlike?
2. 1 Timothy 4:7 says to *train yourself for godliness* (ESV). How do you do this?
3. If Christ is your standard, how are you measuring up? Explain.

Day 5: Commitment – John 6:67

1. How would you define the commitment level of Christians in America versus Christians in a persecuted area of the world? Why is there a difference?
2. Do you find it hard to be committed to the things of Christ daily? What makes it so challenging?
3. What's keeping you from being more committed to Christ? How can you firm up your commitment?

MECHANICS OF
GRACE

DAY I MECHANICS OF GRACE
RECEIVE FORGIVENESS

"He himself bore our sins" in his body on the cross, so that we might die to sin and live for righteousness; "by his wounds you have been healed." —1 Peter 2:24 (NIV)

The key component to gift giving is for the one being given the gift to receive it. I'm sure there was a time in your life when you gave someone a gift and it was not received in the way you expected. I know a young man who was interested in a girl. On Valentine's Day he gave her flowers at school. She took the flowers from him, walked around the corner of the hallway, and threw them in the trash! Later that same day, not knowing that his school crush had thrown away his gift, he was walking down that hallway and noticed the gift he had given her had not been received well. It crushed him! In gift giving, if the desired gift is not received, then what good is the gift at all, outside of the thought?

The act of receiving a gift is not always as easy as accepting a perishable gift. Let me explain it this way. Tony McMullen with Free in Christ Ministries is a good friend of mine who understands this fact all too well. To make a long story short, when Tony was 18 years old and newly married, a drug deal went bad in Tulsa, Oklahoma. He shot his best friend with a shotgun. As a result, he was sent to prison. Tony was angry and full of hatred for the crime he had committed that day in Tulsa. He thought that he would never be able to receive forgiveness for what he had done. Tony could not understand how his friends, family, wife, or even his own kids could ever forgive him. As the Lord would have it, Tony met a man in prison who led him to Christ. As Tony grew in his faith he learned the power of 1 Peter 2:24 – *He himself bore our sins' in his body on the cross, so that we might die to sins and live for righteousness; 'by his wounds you have been healed* (NIV).

To receive the forgiveness of his sins, Tony had to first surrender his life to Jesus Christ, and then realize that Jesus paid for his sin on the cross. Martin Luther once wrote: "All the prophets did foresee in Spirit that Christ should become the greatest transgressor, murderer, adulterer, thief, rebel, blasphemer, etc., that ever was or could be in all the world. For he, being made a sacrifice for the sins of the whole world, is not now an innocent person and without sins...but a sinner. Our most merciful Father...sent his only Son into the world and laid upon Him...the sins of all men saying: Be thou Peter that denier; Paul that persecutor, blasphemer and cruel oppressor; David that adulterer; that sinner which did eat that apple in Paradise; that thief which hanged upon the cross; and briefly be thou the person which had committed the sins of all men; see therefore that thou pay and satisfy for them. Here now comes the law and saith: I find him a sinner... therefore let him die upon the cross. And so he setteth upon him and killeth him. By this means the whole world is purged and cleansed from all sins."[14]

With rebellious hearts, sin is committed, but Christ died to bring forgiveness. Today you can have confidence that you have been forgiven! Stop for a moment and let that sentence sink in. You have been forgiven! When Christ died on the cross He took on all the sins of the world! We have been forgiven of our sins, but we must repent and receive His forgiveness. What good is the gift of forgiveness if you never receive it? Those of you who have never received the forgiveness of Christ will never find rest. The cross is simply a historical act if you do not receive the grace that is available to you because of it. Today, recognize when Christ hung on the cross He was doing it for you and me.

⊕ CONSISTENCY ———

1. Thank Jesus: Take time to pray and thank Jesus for taking your sins on the cross.

2. Receive forgiveness: We have all have sinned and disobeyed God. Accept God's forgiveness today and move forward in His cleansing. While all your sin against God is wiped away, there may be some wrongs you've committed against others you need to seek their forgiveness for. Take steps to reconcile those relationships. There may be other deep hurts within your own heart that you need to deal with as you move forward. Seek the help of your pastor or Christian counselor as you work through these hurts.

3. Don't keep sinning: Some might say, "Well, if God has already forgiven me and all I have to do is receive His grace, then I can keep on sinning." Romans 6:1-2 says it best: *What should we say then? Should we continue in sin so that grace may multiply? Absolutely not! How can we who died to sin still live in it?* Paul continued his line of argument throughout verses 3-13. I encourage you to stop and read that passage right now. Now, finish in verse 14: *For sin will not rule over you, because you are not under law but under grace.* Our lives should be lived differently than the world because of the grace our Lord has given to us. Grace has not given us permission to sin more but to live differently in the power of Christ!

4. Be still and reflect on what Christ did for you on the cross. Taking time to meditate on Christ's great sacrifice will help us remain grateful for His grace.

DAY 2 MECHANICS OF GRACE

GIVE FORGIVENESS

And whenever you stand praying, forgive, if you have anything against anyone, so that your Father also who is in heaven may forgive you your trespasses. —Mark 11:25 (ESV)

Our ability to share forgiveness with others is directly associated with our understanding of the gospel. An improper view of salvation and redemption will produce an improper response to others, no matter the circumstances. If we have a proper view of the gospel, then it will be easier for us to respond in a proper manner toward others. Grace for others' shortcomings is based on our ability to filter God's grace for us. If our view of the gospel is shallow, then it will be very difficult to embrace others' shortcomings. We should forgive as He forgave us: *Be kind to one another, tenderhearted, forgiving one another, as God in Christ forgave you* (Eph. 4:32, ESV).

Yesterday's focus was on understanding the grace that God has given us. Today's focus is applying that grace to others. It will be nearly impossible to share forgiveness with others if we are not constantly growing in our understanding of the gospel. Without a proper knowledge of what Jesus has accomplished on the cross it will become increasingly difficult to share that extent of love toward others. Most of the time, our frustration with others first starts with a distorted view of ourselves. If we think too highly of ourselves, then it will become natural to think low of everyone else. A distorted view of ourselves will cause a distorted view of our brothers in Christ. Jesus said we first need a clear view of ourselves: *Why do you see the speck that is in your brother's eye, but do not notice the log that is in your own eye? Or how can you say to your brother, "Let me take the speck out of your eye,' when there is the log in your own eye? You hypocrite, first take the log out of your own eye, and then you will see clearly to*

71

take the speck out of your brother's eye (Matt. 7:3-5, ESV).

Many young believers struggle with accepting their own faults. They are quick to blame others, but slow in identifying themselves as the root problem. Any time there is a conflict with you and someone else, remember that all conflicts involve at least two people. Now, I am not saying that you are necessarily the person to blame in every situation. But, take a minute to realize that there is one reoccurring theme in your conflicts with others: you. If you are at constant tension with others, then you must first examine yourself as the root cause. Step one in fixing any problem is identifying the root cause.

How do we change? The goal is not to avoid conflict. Rather, it is to resolve conflict and strive to live at peace with all men. Paul said, *If possible, so far as it depends on you, live peaceably with all* (Rom. 12:18, ESV). It is impossible to avoid conflict. Inevitably, we will upset someone in some way. How we choose to respond will make all the difference. Reminding ourselves of the forgiveness we have found through the cross will allow us to approach our brothers in Christ with forgiveness. Reflecting upon the cross should move us to respond with grace and forgiveness toward those who have wounded us.

Jesus clearly set the standard for forgiveness when Peter inquired about how many times he should forgive someone in Matthew 18:21-22: *Then Peter came to Him and said, "Lord, how many times could my brother sin against me and I forgive him? As many as seven times?" "I tell you, not as many as seven," Jesus said to him, "but 70 times seven."*

Jesus followed the statement with a parable describing how a slave owed an enormous debt to the king. When the king came to collect, the slave had no way to pay the debt and begged for more time. The king was compassionate and forgave the debt. However, the forgiven slave went out and found a fellow slave who owed him a small amount. He demanded the debt be paid. When the fellow slaved begged for more time, the forgiven slave showed no compassion and threw him into prison. Other slaves saw what had happened and reported the incident to the king, who summoned the forgiven slave: *You wicked slave! I forgave you all that debt because you begged me. Shouldn't you also have had mercy on your fellow slave, as I had mercy on you?' And his master got angry and handed him over to the jailers to be tortured until he could pay everything that was owed. So My heavenly Father will also do to you if each of you does not forgive his brother from his heart* (Matt. 18:32-35).

We who have been forgiven much, must also love others with a forgiving heart.

⊗ CONSISTENCY ───────

1) Strive to resolve conflict immediately. The longer you allow an issue or conflict to go unresolved, the harder it will be to forgive others. Paul said for us not to let our anger linger: *In your anger do not sin: Do not let the sun go down while you are still angry* (Eph. 4:26, NIV).

When you are offended by someone, don't be afraid to share with them what you are feeling. Most of the time, people are not aware of their shortcomings. Be honest with others, but do not use this as an opportunity to call others out in their sin. Rather, pray to God about any shortcomings in your life. Then you can approach your brother in grace and resolve any conflict you may have with him. Prayer is the key to resolving conflict. Without prayer it will be difficult to approach others with a sincere heart full of grace and truth. Take this to heart: *If possible, so far as it depends on you, live peaceably with all* (Rom. 12:18, ESV).

2) Choose to forgive. No one said that forgiving others would be easy. Rather, it is a daily decision to love others unconditionally. Follow Christ's example and be willing to forgive those who wrong you. As we noted earlier: *Be kind and compassionate to one another, forgiving each other, just as in Christ God forgave you* (Eph. 4:32, NIV).

DAY 3 MECHANICS OF GRACE
EVERY DAY IS A NEW DAY

But if it is by grace, it is no longer on the basis of works; otherwise grace would no longer be grace. —Romans 11:6 (ESV)

Life is a journey and the paths that you take on this journey are left up to you. We are born sinners. The Bible says in Romans 3:23, *For all have sinned and fall short of the glory of God* (NIV). According to Romans 6:23, the result of sin is eternal death. Sin equals eternal death and separation from God, but God, loving those whom He created, moved to redeem His people back to Himself. John 3:16 tells us that God sent His only Son, Jesus, to die for our sins so that we would not perish but have everlasting life. This verse also signifies that Jesus is a gift to us. The key to all gifts is that we have a choice to receive them or reject them. God has given you the ability to choose to receive His gift, Jesus, or to reject His gift. When you come to the point where you receive God's gift, you have come to the point of total surrender of your life. Paul says it like this in Galatians 2:20, *I have been crucified with Christ and I no longer live, but Christ lives in me. The life I now live in the body, I live by faith in the Son of God, who loved me and gave himself for me* (NIV). This first moment of salvation is called *justification*. Through Christ's sacrifice and His shed blood we are justified before God. We are completely cleansed from sin and take on the righteousness of Jesus. The next stage of our spiritual journey with Christ is called *sanctification*. At its most basic form sanctification is the process of becoming more like Christ. Pastor John Piper says it this way: "(Sanctification is) progressively becoming like Jesus. Gradually becoming like Jesus, or becoming holy. Becoming conformed to the image of Christ. Little by little, over time — from conversion till Jesus comes back, or you die — you are in the process of sanctification, becoming sanctified, becoming holy."[15]

Paul provides a description of sanctification in Romans 6:6-14: *For we know that our old self was crucified with Him in order that sin's dominion over the body may be abolished, so that we may no longer be enslaved to sin, since a person who has died is freed from sin's claims. Now if we died with Christ, we believe that we will also live with Him, because we know that Christ, having been raised from the dead, will not die again. Death no longer rules over Him. For in light of the fact that He died, He died to sin once for all; but in light of the fact that He lives, He lives to God. So, you too consider yourselves dead to sin but alive to God in Christ Jesus. Therefore do not let sin reign in your mortal body, so that you obey its desires. And do not offer any parts of it to sin as weapons for unrighteousness. But as those who are alive from the dead, offer yourselves to God, and all the parts of yourselves to God as weapons for righteousness. For sin will not rule over you, because you are not under law but under grace.*

God's grace saves us and by the power of the Holy Spirit we are forever changed. Then we begin the journey of growing spiritually to look like Jesus, which is sanctification. The inward change results in holy living. The Bible says in Luke 6:45, *A good man brings good things out of the good stored up in his heart, and an evil man brings evil things out of the evil stored up in his heart. For the mouth speaks what the heart is full of* (NIV). Our lives portray our heart's desire.

Remember this is a journey. On all journeys, there are ups and downs. The process of sanctification is a journey through life toward Jesus. Even though we know that life will have its mountaintop moments and its valleys, we should still strive to be perfect. We know we will strike out at times—we will shoot an air ball, we will hit our shins on the box jumps, we will miss that note—but it doesn't mean that we give up. We grow by learning and as we all know, we learn through failure as much as through success. So what do we do now? When we sin, we repent. We turn 180 degrees back to Christ and learn from our failures. We are called to repent of our sin, which means to turn from it and go a different direction. For the one who has surrendered his life to Christ, sin no longer separates him from Christ, yet it can push him off the path of sanctification. When you sin, repent and move forward!

The challenge today is for you to recognize that life is a journey toward Christ and it takes intentional living to become more like Him. Remember that sanctification is not a "works-based faith." It is a life that is committed to holiness. Men, we must walk the path of sanctification on a daily basis. The challenge to do the common uncommonly well has never been a challenge of ease but a challenge to holiness. Today's reading takes you to this level.

 CONSISTENCY ———

1. Journal. Journal, either in a notebook or use the app "maxjournal." Write what hinders the sanctification process in your life. What sin most often takes you off the journey to be like Christ? List it, then confess and repent of it. Pray that God gives you the strength to run from it the next time you face that temptation.

2. Read Romans 6:6-14 one more time. Read it slowly, highlighting and underling aspects of the passage that stand out to you.

3. Breathe in God's grace. Many might read this and say, "Man, I'm terrible at this whole Christianity thing." Remember it is not about what you do! It is about what Christ has done! We all need this reminder to stop and recognize that *while we were still sinners, Christ died for us* (Rom. 5:8). Remember that we have a faithful God that will never leave us or forsake us. He is always with us. Through all of our junk, stupidity, and unfaithfulness, He remains constant. Remember that the grace of God does not give us permission to continue living in sin, but His mercies are new every day.

DAY 4 MECHANICS OF GRACE
EVERY MOUNTAIN HAS A VALLEY

Even though I walk through the valley of the shadow of death, I will fear no evil, for you are with me; your rod and your staff, they comfort me. —Psalm 23:4 (ESV)

Every mountaintop has a valley. Our Christian faith will experience both good and bad seasons of life. The mountaintops and valleys don't necessarily correlate with our closeness to God. Sometimes trials take us to the lowest spots, but it's in those moments when we most closely sense the presence of God. Also, trials and circumstances are intended to grow and mature us as believers: *Count it all joy, my brothers, when you meet trials of various kinds, for you know that the testing of your faith produces steadfastness. And let steadfastness have its full effect, that you may be perfect and complete, lacking in nothing* (Jas. 1:2-4, ESV). Many believers shy away from challenging situations. They fear failing. But often, it's in the challenges we face where God wants to teach us.

Up to this point we have talked a great deal about discipline and grace and how we need both to grow as believers. Today's focus is to remind us that we cannot mature as believers on our own. Ultimately, God is sovereign and always knows what is best for us. Many times we try to do things on our own, and He graciously gives a humble reminder of who is in control. Every season of life has a purpose. Our responsibility in every season of life is to identify that purpose.

No one ever said that the Christian faith would be glamorous. The disciples knew this firsthand. Jesus told His disciples: *"If the world hates you, understand that it hated Me before it hated you. If you were of the world, the world would love you as its own. However, because you are not of the world, but I have chosen you out of it, the world hates you. Remember the word I spoke to you: 'A slave is not greater* than *his master.' If they persecuted Me, they will also persecute you"* (John 15:18-20a). The same still holds true for us today. If we desire to live a godly lifestyle, then we will face persecution at some point in our faith. Persecution looks radically different now than it did two thousand years ago. If you were caught following Christ during Jesus' time, the consequence could be death. Look no further than the stoning of Stephen (Acts 7:54-60). While that kind of treatment is still the case for many believers all over the world, it's not the norm in America. For us, following Jesus may only cost us some ridicule or being socially ostracized.

Unfortunately, some Christians live as if that cost is too high. But we need to remember that God often uses those circumstances and trials we face to transform us into the godly men He has called us to be. We need to be able to say: *For I am not ashamed of the gospel, for it is the power of God for salvation to everyone who believes, to the Jew first and also to the Greek* (Rom. 1:16, ESV). Yes, it could possibly cost you your starting position on the team or maybe that girl you are trying to impress. But following Jesus in our current society will cost you far less than what His disciples were willing to sacrifice—their lives. Honestly ask yourself, what do you have to lose? Jesus and His disciples risked it all. How far are you willing to go to follow Him?

Jesus made it clear that following Him was an all or nothing proposition: *If anyone would come after me, let him deny himself and take up his cross daily and follow me. For whoever would save his life will lose it, but whoever loses his life for my sake will save it. For what does it profit a man if he gains the whole world and loses or forfeits himself? For whoever is ashamed of me and of my words, of him will the Son of Man be ashamed when he comes in his glory and the glory of the Father and of the holy angels* (Luke 9:23-26, ESV).

We cannot grow as believers unless we embrace the trials God has placed in our lives. Every mountain has a valley, and those who grow and mature in their faith embrace difficult circumstances as an opportunity to grow closer to Christ. We must stop running from the cross (suffering and persecution of the faith), and in turn run to the cross (embracing any challenge that God places in our lives), so that we may be tested and strengthened in our faith. God's Word assures us that we will not suffer in vain: *Blessed is the man who remains steadfast under trial, for when he has stood the test he will receive the crown of life, which God has promised to those who love him* (Jas. 1:12, ESV). For those faithful men who stay the course, God promises a faithful reward.

⊗ CONSISTENCY ———

1) Challenge yourself. Embrace any valley that God may place in your life: *Count it all joy, my brothers, when you meet trials of various kinds, for you know that the testing of your faith produces steadfastness. And let steadfastness have its full effect, that you may be perfect and complete, lacking in nothing* (Jas. 1:2-4, ESV).

Remember that God's purpose for you may take you through storms. You may not understand God's will in that time, but you can rest assured that God is in control. He promises to never leave you or forsake you. Watch to see how God uses that storm to transform your life and possibly impact someone else's life.

2) Run to God's Word. As a godly man, you will find rest and satisfaction in God's Word. When faced with a trial, God's Word will bring strength, comfort, and guidance.

3) Surround yourself with godly men. Encouragement can be found in the council of godly men: *Where there is no guidance, a people falls, but in an abundance of counselors there is safety* (Prov. 11:14, ESV). Having godly men in your life can save you from making bad decisions when faced with challenging situations. They can help steer you toward Scripture and away from the world. Make sure this band of brothers is godly and their intentions are to point you closer to Christ.

DAY 5 MECHANICS OF GRACE
DEPENDENCE

I am the vine; you are the branches. Whoever abides in me and I in him, he it is that bears much fruit, for apart from me you can do nothing. —John 15:5 (ESV)

We will forever be in need of God's grace. His grace is necessary for forgiveness as well as growth. Many people strive for self-dependence in every aspect of their lives, but spiritual growth is found by those who choose to trust in God's grace instead of their own strength.

As a young Arkansas boy, Brian was captivated by snow skiing. He dreamed of going down the mountains of Colorado at high speeds. He worked hard every day and saved up money so that he could live out his dream. Finally the day came when Brian had saved enough money. Eager to get on the slopes, he made all the necessary arrangements and purchases. Once arriving at the bottom of the mountain with new boots, skies, and clothes, he was puzzled at how he could reach the top of the mountain. The mountain was very steep and covered in four feet of snow. It seemed almost impossible to climb. However, passionate about his dream, he started the journey to the top. After six hours of plowing through the snow, he managed to only make it two hundred meters. Tired and frustrated, he was ready to give up. He started his journey back to the bottom and made a sudden surprise. The ski lifts were only a hundred meters away from his starting point.

How many people can relate to Brian? Oftentimes in life we try to work as hard as possible to find results. Passionate about different things in life, we will take all the necessary measures to achieve our goals. Spiritual growth does not work in that manner. Instead, there is an easier way. The ski lifts in the story were a representation of God's grace. Many people have spiritually abandoned the ski lifts in hopes of reaching the top of the mountain on their own. However, it is impossible to reach the top on our own. God wants us to continue to be dependent on Him. His Word says, *For apart from me you can do nothing* (John 15:5, ESV).

Grace, discipline, and spiritual growth are inseparable. If we lose sight of grace, we can easily form a legalistic mindset. It will be about keeping the rules and what we can do in our own power. The Pharisees lived with this mindset. They would study God's Word all day long, and share how "spiritual" they were with others. But Jesus said this about the Pharisees: *You search the Scriptures because you think that in them you have eternal life; and it is they that bear witness about me, yet you refuse to come to me that you may have life* (John 5:39-40, ESV). Consumed by their own performance and pride, they failed to recognize that Jesus Himself was the ultimate source of life. They worked so hard, yet failed to accept Jesus' simple message of, *"I am the way, and the truth, and the life. No one comes to the Father except through me"* (John 14:6, ESV). The truth is that we can work hard to grow as believers, but without accepting Jesus as the ultimate source of life we will fail. Being spiritually disciplined is a great thing. However, we must balance discipline with grace.

Sometimes taking the ski lifts is the hardest thing to do. Being dependent on someone else is very uncomfortable. Many of us would rather plow through the snow for hours instead of admit we need God. The truth is that we will only get as far as God allows us to go. No amount of talent or hard work will replace what God is able to do: *For by grace you have been saved through faith. And this is not your own doing; it is the gift of God, not a result of works, so that no one may boast* (Eph. 2:8-9, ESV). Apart from God, our hard work and labor are in vain. *Unless the LORD builds the house, those who build it labor in vain. Unless the LORD watches over the city, the watchman stays awake in vain. It is in vain that you rise up early and go late to rest, eating the bread of anxious toil; for he gives to his beloved sleep* (Ps. 127:1-2, ESV). Dependence can be uncomfortable, but when we lean on God, He does much greater things than we can do on our own.

Now to him who is able to do far more abundantly than all that we ask or think (Eph. 3:20, ESV). We as believers just need to simply trust in Him and His ways. The only way we can get where we want to go spiritually is by choosing to sit on His ski lift of grace.

⊗ CONSISTENCY ———

1) **Depend on Christ.** Do you find yourself trying to earn your significance as a believer? Maybe you understand and accept God's grace, but you struggle with depending upon Him. If this is the case, then read John 15:1-11. Remind yourself that Jesus said, *Apart from me you can do nothing* (John 15:5, ESV).

2) **Commit to memorize the following passages:**
I am the vine; you are the branches. Whoever abides in me and I in him, he it is that bears much fruit, for apart from me you can do nothing. —John 15:5 (ESV)

For by grace you have been saved through faith. And this is not your own doing; it is the gift of God, not a result of works, so that no one may boast. —Ephesians 2:8-9 (ESV)

3) **Consider reading** *Discipline of Grace* **by Jerry Bridges.** This book provides a good understanding of how to balance God's grace with our discipline. We need both to grow as believers.

DAY 6 MECHANICS OF GRACE

INTENSITY

While most believers know about grace, some struggle to implement it in their lives. They affirm the concept of grace while continuing to walk in a works-based faith, striving to gain God's approval through their goodness. This also affects their relationships with others. The better we understand the grace God has displayed toward us, the better we will be at showing grace to others. There is no better picture of grace than that which was given through the gospel: *For while we were still weak, at the right time Christ died for the ungodly. For one will scarcely die for a righteous person—though perhaps for a good person one would dare even to die—but God shows his love for us in that while we were still sinners, Christ died for us* (Rom. 5:6-8, ESV). Grace first starts in our vertical relationship with God, and then is displayed in our horizontal relationship with others. Without an ongoing and maturing relationship with God, it will be very difficult to share grace with others. Our ability to forgive others of their shortcomings will depend on our ability to understand our own shortcomings and God's forgiveness in our lives.

Grace is a concept that society in general struggles to understand. Our culture is driven by a works-based performance. If you do X, then you will get Y. This applies to our work, sports, and life in general. However, the basis of the gospel is not dependent on your ability to perform. Instead, it is based on your ability to understand your sinfulness and God's holiness, and how Jesus was able to bridge the gap through His death, burial, and resurrection. Understanding what Jesus accomplished on the cross allows us to be open about our sinfulness and marvel at God's holiness. Without a clear view of the gospel, we will forever feel enslaved by a works-based salvation that will never satisfy. There are many things you can work hard for in life. However, eternal life is a free gift that has been given by God and cannot be earned. As Paul said: *For by grace you have been saved through faith. And this is not your own doing; it is the gift of God, not a result of works, so that no one may boast* (Eph. 2:8-9, ESV).

Day 1: Receive Forgiveness – 1 Peter 2:24

1. Why do some people struggle to receive God's forgiveness? Have you ever found yourself in that place?
2. Does knowing that Christ will forgive us give us permission to keep sinning? Explain.
3. What is the appropriate response to someone forgiving you?

Day 2: Give Forgiveness – Mark 11:25

1. How hard is it to forgive someone who has wronged you?
2. Do you have anyone you need to forgive that you have not done so yet? Explain. What's keeping you from forgiving them?

Day 3: Every Day Is a New Day – Romans 11:6

1. Is it possible to start every day fresh? Explain.
2. What is sanctification?
3. What steps are you taking daily to become more like Christ?

Day 4: Every Mountain Has a Valley – Psalm 23:4

1. Have you ever hit a valley in your life or walk with Christ? Explain the valley you walked through and how you came out of it.
2. What trials do you face daily?
3. Who are some men in your life that help you through the valley?

Day 5: Dependence – John 15:5

1. Have you ever had to depend on someone else in order to make it through a certain situation? Explain.
2. How would you define the grace of God?
3. Do you struggle to extend grace to others? Why or why not?

MECHANICS OF DISCIPLESHIP

DAY 1 MECHANICS OF DISCIPLESHIP
INVESTMENT

And let us consider how we may spur one another on toward love and good deeds. —Hebrews 10:24 (NIV)

Have you ever started a workout plan without a coach or friend pushing you to complete it? If so, it is almost certain that at some point you thought, "I don't want to do this today." That thought, along with no accountability, caused you to skip that day's workout. Just one missed workout creates a mental block that makes it even harder to get up the next day to work out, and before you know it, you are days behind where you needed to be. One of the keys to having a successful day-to-day workout is to find someone who cares enough about you to push you and keep you accountable to your workout plan. This person could be a coach, friend, co-worker, or maybe even a parent. No matter their relationship to you, they say, "I care enough about you that I am going to push you to be better." Eventually this person who has taken a personal investment in your life can become your mentor. According to Merriam-Webster, a mentor is "someone who teaches or gives help and advice to a less experienced and often younger person." I believe that men have forgotten the need to be a mentor to those who look up to us. Today's culture is calling for more men to mentor the next generation.

Hebrews 10:24 begins with this statement: *and let us consider* (NIV). The author challenged his readers to give some thought as to how they could exhort and encourage one another. When considering God's call on our lives, it's important that we recognize God's divine strength within us. From my experience, most people say no to God's call on their life to equip others simply because they think they have nothing to give. Receive today what Jesus said to His disciples right before He was taken up to heaven in Acts 1:8: *But you will receive power when the Holy Spirit comes on you; and you will be my witnesses in Jerusalem, and in all Judea and Samaria, and to the ends of the earth* (NIV).

All mentors must recognize that it is only through the power of the Holy Spirit that we have the ability to help equip someone else to live as a devoted follower of Christ.

The next part of this verse in Hebrews tells us what we are to consider. We are to consider "how we may spur one another on." It is no secret that life is difficult with its ups and downs. Continuing this journey of life with great zeal and passion depends greatly on whom we surround ourselves with. God strategically uses others to inspire us so that we keep running the race that we are called to run. As you are reading this, I want you to ask yourself two simple questions: Who is in my life that is spurring me on, and who am I spurring on?

We have considered the challenge to spur one another on but what are we to spur them on to? The writer of Hebrews articulates that we are to spur one another on "toward love and good deeds." Guys, we need to be challenging other guys to live according to the Scriptures. We need young men of love, not hate. We need young men who make wise choices, not choices that will cost them their reputation. We probably all have been in that situation when all the guys around us are daring us to do something stupid and we cave to their pressure. We typically get ourselves into trouble when this happens. I want to challenge you to run from the voices in your life that are pushing you away from love and good deeds and run to the voices that spur you on toward holiness.

More boys are growing up without fathers than ever before. As a result, these young men are growing up with no father figure spurring them on to love and good deeds. If you're a teenage guy reading this and you are one of the many without that godly father figure in your life, I encourage you to find a godly man to be a mentor to you. Pray and ask God to bring that person into your life. Talk with your student pastor or pastor about the situation and let them speak to the situation. Perhaps they might be willing to mentor you, or point you to another man who could be your mentor. If you're an adult man who grew up without a father figure, instead of focusing on the negative and all the hurt that has brought you, choose to focus on becoming that godly father figure for someone else. If you're a guy that has that godly figure in your life who is spurring you on, how are you paying it forward? Who are you mentoring and giving out what you are receiving in that process? You are called to empower the next generation for the gospel of Jesus Christ, no matter your background or age. May we spur on the next generation toward love and good deeds.

 CONSISTENCY ————

1. Take steps to be a mentor. If you're an older teenage guy or an adult man, write down five names of guys younger than you that you could begin mentoring by taking them through this book. When you finish this 8-week experience with them, continue the journey by leading them through *Checkpoints: A Tactical Guide to Manhood.* That would give you 80 days of guided talks to start your mentoring process.

2. Create a band of brothers. List the men in your life who are pushing you toward love and good deeds. If you have none, make a list of men you would like to be speaking into your life. After you do this, ask them if they would be interested in investing in your spiritual life.

3. Give thanks. If you have had men pour into your life, contact them and thank them for helping you in this way.

DAY 2 MECHANICS OF DISCIPLESHIP

BALANCE

Do not be conformed to this world, but be transformed by the renewal of your mind, that by testing you may discern what is the will of God, what is good and acceptable and perfect. —Romans 12:2 (ESV)

As we grow into disciple makers, the tendency at times will be to give too much attention to helping others while we let our own spiritual life run dry. We must remain aware of our constant need to be filled by God's Spirit and grow in Him.

By God's grace I have been blessed with a job teaching people how to eat healthy and exercise in a way that will transform their lives. As much as I enjoy my job, I must remind myself that my word loses credibility if I am not being transformed myself. If I am not displaying the very mechanics that I am teaching others to live by, then my words will lose their impact. One of my toughest challenges with being on the CrossFit seminar staff is balancing my fitness while encouraging others to pursue theirs. It requires a lot of discipline and sacrifice to live that balanced lifestyle as an athlete and coach. People need to see the transformation happening in your life before they can begin to trust you with their lives. The spiritual journey of discipleship is very similar.

Discipleship requires us to lead by example. Embrace the words of the apostle Paul, who says: *Be imitators of me, as I am of Christ* (1 Cor. 11:1, ESV). In Paul's process of challenging believers to step up to the plate and grow in their faith, he was first accepting the challenge of growing in his faith. Notice that Paul fixed his eyes on Christ while challenging others to fix their eyes on him. Someone once gave a beautiful illustration of our goal as believers and disciple makers. The goal is to become like a piece of glass that is in between a person and the Grand Canyon. When people see the Grand Canyon (resembling Christ), they are not consumed by the piece of glass (resembling us as disciple makers) standing in between them and the Grand Canyon. They become captivated by the beauty of the Grand Canyon (Christ). The only way that someone will notice the piece of glass is if it is dirty, stained, or preventing the sight of the Grand Canyon. We realize that every disciple maker will have some form of stain or dirt on their glass, at times. But as we grow, our goal is not to noticed. Rather, it is to become more invisible so that others can see the beauty of Christ more clearly. It requires us to continually put off our old self and embrace the new self created in Christ. As Paul said: *You were taught, with regard to your former way of life, to put off your old self, which is being corrupted by its deceitful desires; to be made new in the attitude of your minds; and to put on the new self, created to be like God in true righteousness and holiness* (Eph. 4:22-24, NIV). Paul is not trying to make much of himself in challenging others to follow him. Rather, his goal was to become invisible so that others can see the beauty of our Savior.

As you grow to lead other guys, they need to see the transformation of your life first and foremost. It will be very difficult finding the balance of feeding others while constantly feeding yourself.

One of my favorite moments in our level one CrossFit seminar is at the closing, where we challenge our participants to make the transformation from athlete to coach. We explain that just because someone is a great athlete doesn't necessarily mean they will be a great coach. No one becomes a great athlete overnight. Rather, they train themselves and put in the hard work. The same holds true for coaching. It takes time and you learn much through trial and error. You might even consider yourself a bad coach at the start, but keep learning and growing. Know that you will make mistakes. Learn from them and move forward. Ask for forgiveness and be humble enough to show others that you are learning during the process. Finally, make sure you take time to refuel yourself. Your ability to keep growing as you pour into others is a key to being a productive disciple-maker.

 ## CONSISTENCY ———

1) Help others grow. If you have a desire to pour into the lives of others, there has to be a transition from focusing on just growing yourself to helping others grow, as the apostle Paul told Timothy: *and what you have heard from me in the presence of many witnesses entrust to faithful men who will be able to teach others also* (2 Tim. 2:2, ESV).

2) Be balanced. As you pour into others, it is essential that you continue to grow yourself. No disciple maker will be successful if they do not take the time to first fuel their own spiritual growth.

3) Realize it is a process. You will make mistakes along the way, but ask for forgiveness and stay humble while you lead others.

Here are three essential actions to help you be an effective disciple-maker:

1) Spend time in God's Word to fuel yourself. You cannot forsake your own personal spiritual growth.
2) Continue to allow a godly man to speak into your life. Even as you lead others, continue to value the input of a mentor.
3) Lead by example. Remember that if your life doesn't match your words, you will fail as a leader. You will make mistakes along the way, but ask for forgiveness and choose to stay humble while you lead other men.

In order to be an effective disciple maker you must balance the following three areas.

1) Spend time in God's Word to fuel yourself.
2) Spend intentional time with men you want to lead and have intentional spiritual conversations.
3) Continue to stay humble and remember that the goal of a disciple maker is to point the men you lead to the gospel and not yourself.

DAY 3 MECHANICS OF DISCIPLESHIP
INFLUENCERS

Make every effort to live in peace with everyone and to be holy; without holiness no one will see the Lord. —Hebrews 12:14 (NIV)

Leadership guru John Maxwell has coined the phrase: "Leadership is influence. Nothing more nothing less."[16] Even though this seems like a simple concept to understand, it is difficult for guys to grasp. Typically, we as men seem to buy into this belief that leadership is positional in nature. Furthermore, we believe that if we are "cooler" than everyone else or if we have earned the privilege as team captain, first chair, or even president of a corporation, we, by default, are to be considered the leader. The problem with these "positions of leadership" is that people don't always follow these leaders. Those who lead only by position never really effectively lead. I want to challenge you to be a different kind of leader. I want to challenge you to be a "Holy Leader." A Holy Leader is 100 percent committed to the calling of God on his life instead of trying to earn people's approval. Being holy never equates to being cool; being holy equates to righteous living. Our culture needs men who are more concerned about their holiness rather than their popularity.

Influential leaders set themselves apart from the crowd. Their lives of character and integrity rise above the rest. They are the ones in front of the crowd leading the way, but they are never too far away that they lose the crowd. They don't revel in their position, but take the role of a servant, leading with humble strength. At times you will not find them at the top of the organizational chart but in the "middle of the pack." I believe the reason for this is that the leader at the top got lost in positional leadership and as a result people stopped following.

If you want to be an influential leader let me challenge you today from the Word of God: *Make every effort to live in peace with everyone and to be holy; without holiness no one will see the Lord* (Heb. 12:14, NIV). Live a life of holiness and you will be respected. A life of holiness is a life set apart from the world. One who lives a life of holiness seeks not to please people but to please the Lord. His life is marked by obedience and a deep desire to reflect Christ in everything he does. He turns away from worldly popularity and is committed to what he believes. He chooses to follow Jesus no matter what the crowd says.

Through the years, the guys with the most spiritual influence have been the ones who lived out what they say they believed. They lived lives that were worth following.

It's important to note that this does not mean you are perfect. As a matter of fact, it means you realize you are far from perfect, and that you are totally dependent upon the grace and power of Christ. You take seriously the weight of responsibility as a leader and guard yourself from compromise. You realize that as an influencer your life is on display and you make a concerted effort to live with character. You understand that while it may take a long time to move into a position of influence, one bad decision made in a split second can cause you to lose it all.

Every person has some sphere of influence, including you. Take seriously the position you are in as you point others to Jesus.

⊕ CONSISTENCY ———

1. Self-Evaluate. Consider your sphere of influence. Would you say you're being a positive influence on those around you? Why or why not? What needs to change in your life to better influence people toward Jesus?

2. Accept the Challenge of Holiness. Holiness means to be set apart. It does not mean you become a loner and never talk to anyone again.

It means you live your life differently than the rest of the world. Take seriously the call to live a life of holiness.

3. Memorize Scripture. One key to holy living and spiritual strength is living by the Word of God. As the psalmist stated in Psalm 119:11, *I have hidden your word in my heart that I might not sin against you* (NIV).

Start today by memorizing 1 Peter 1:15-16: *But as the One who called you is holy, you also are to be holy in all your conduct; for it is written, Be holy, because I am holy.* Every day get up and pray, "Lord let me live out 1 Peter 1:16 today and be an influencer for you."

DAY 4 MECHANICS OF DISCIPLESHIP
ACCOUNTABILITY

Bear one another's burdens, and so fulfill the law of Christ.
—Galatians 6:2 (ESV)

Holding yourself and others to a standard is essential. It is difficult to mature as a believer without some set form of accountability. God never designed for us to embrace the Christian faith alone. We as believers should look no further than the fact that God is a Trinitarian God. That means God the Father, God the Son (Jesus), and God the Holy Spirit all dwell in perfect community with each other. God is three in one, and there is no separating them. If God lives in perfect union and accountability, how much more do we as believers need to follow His example?

Accountability is essential in finding long-lasting results in so many areas of your life. No matter what you desire to accomplish in this lifetime, you must establish a form of accountability to achieve it. Every great employer has a boss or clients, every great athlete has a coach and teammates, and every Olympic gold medalist had training partners. It is impossible to completely separate yourself from other human beings. But even if you could, it would be a very foolish decision. No one ever achieved great things on their own.

God did not design for us to be alone. His Word clearly states: *Two are better than one, because they have a good reward for their toil. For if they fall, one will lift up his fellow. But woe to him who is alone when he falls and has not another to lift him up* (Eccl. 4:9-10, ESV). We need other men in our lives to pick us up when times get hard. We need men in our lives who will challenge us to do things when we become complacent or stagnant in our walk. We need men who are not afraid to tell us when we are wrong. Having a set form of accountability does not mean that you will never go through difficult circumstances. However, it does mean that you do not have to face those hard times alone. Try to think of accountability as having a band of brothers who are ready to fight any battle with you.

There are three things I look for when establishing accountability partners.

I) Is this someone I can trust? This is essential since you will probably be sharing very personal information about yourself with this person. You should have confidence to tell this person anything and know that they will only use this information to build you up. This will also require you to be transparent. It is impossible to have an effective accountability system without trust and transparency.

2) Will they speak truth into my life? We need accountability partners who are not afraid to call us out when we are in the wrong. This requires a large amount of maturity, and must be done in a way that is designed to draw us to repentance. You don't want others to simply identify a fault. Instead, you want someone who can help you see your fault and then help you come up with a solution. Accountability partners are able to identify our sinfulness and then direct us toward Christlikeness.

3) Are they growing closer to Christ? Ultimately, it is impossible for someone who is not growing and maturing in their walk with Christ to point you closer to Christ. If you want to grow in your walk with Christ, then make sure you are establishing an accountability system with maturing believers. You should be able to look at anyone in your accountability group and say, "I wish my walk would look more like _____." Not that you are envious of their walk but rather inspired to draw closer to Christ through their example.

✪ CONSISTENCY ———

1. Assess accountability partners. Do you have accountability partners? If so, share with them all the different ways they have inspired you. If not, make a list of three to five men who would fulfill the three questions above and ask them if they would be willing to hold you accountable.

The following guys possess traits that I would love to have more of in my life. The neat thing is that we all share a passion for CrossFit and Jesus. Therefore, we love to push each other physically and spiritually.

1) Rich Froning—I am inspired by his discipline and perseverance. Anytime I start to feel sorry for myself, Rich is quick to tell me to "man up." No matter the task, you can always count on Rich to give 100 percent.

2) Will Enochs—I am inspired by Will's passion and understanding of the gospel. As a man who discipled me and helped lead me to Christ, he is constantly challenging me to grow closer to Christ through his example. Thanks to Will, I know to never become complacent in my spiritual walk.

3) Zach Oneal—I am inspired by his wisdom. No matter the difficulty of a situation, it seems that Zach always has a solution. Whenever faced with a tough situation, I always know who to call.

4) Tate Rivera—I am inspired by his passion for missions and his willingness to leave the comforts of our society in order to further advance the Kingdom.

5) Elijah Muhammad (aka EZ)—I am inspired by EZ's love for his family. Many people talk about putting their family first, but very few do. One day I hope to love my family the way that he loves his.

No one is perfect, but we all possess different attributes of God and are striving to be more like Christ every day. This is the heart of accountability. May we always have each other's back and be ready to fight the good fight for and with one another.

2. Develop a plan. When meeting with your accountability partners, develop a plan and vision for each meeting. It is one thing to just meet and hang out; it is another thing to meet with purpose. Develop a purpose to your meetings so that you can be held accountable at the highest level. Those who meet with no plan will never develop healthy accountability.

3. Be consistent. The key to great accountability is meeting with guys who are consistent in their walk with Christ and consistently speaking into your life. Do not surround yourself with people who aren't serious about holding you accountable or those who cannot live up to the challenges. Surround yourself with people who will consistently be involved in your life and will live a consistent life for Christ.

DAY 5 MECHANICS OF DISCIPLESHIP
COMMITMENT

For I could wish that I myself were cursed and cut off from Christ for the sake of my people, those of my own race. —Romans 9:3 (NIV)

Paul's anguish for the Jewish people was so strong that he longed to take on their sins so they could go to heaven. "The Jews gloried in the fact that as Israelites they were God's Chosen People (Deut. 7:6; cf. Rom. 2:17–20a; 3:1–2). But now in God's program of salvation in the church, Jewish involvement was decreasing while Gentile participation was becoming dominant."[17] Paul knew his fellow Jews must receive Christ individually into their lives; they would not know Him just because of who they were.

That takes us to why Paul said in verse 3: *For I could wish that I myself were cursed and cut off from Christ for the sake of my people, those of my own race.*

Paul's heart was broken over the lostness of his people. I believe that too many of us have no desire or have lost our desire to be diligent in sharing our faith to win others to Christ. Whether we want to admit it or not, our actions indicate that we are more worried about what others think of us than about where they will spend eternity.

I had the unique privilege of meeting a missionary named Shodankey Johnson in 2014. Pastor Shodankey is considered to be the leader in one of the modern-day movements of Jesus Christ all because of his commitment to reach those who are lost in Africa. Shodankey has been beaten, stoned, and imprisoned, yet each time he is released and set free through the power of Christ. Even though he has been continually persecuted for his faith, he continues to stick to his commitment to Christ and to winning his community and the world to Jesus.

While spending time with him I came to this shattering conclusion: Americans always want to go on mission trips to help others in the world, but what if we are the ones who need missionaries? By seeing a missionary's commitment to Christ we may grasp what it really means to live out the gospel. Guys, I'm afraid that we have lost the passion and urgency that comes with the message of the cross. While Pastor Shodankey is willing to be stoned and beaten for the faith, we balk at something that might take us a little outside our comfort zone.

Where is our commitment level to take the gospel to our community? I wonder about the person who lives next to you, who sits next to you in your classes, who rides the bus with you, or who is on your team, in your band, or in your club. Do those who are around you most even know of your commitment to Christ? Do they know that you are in love with Jesus?

I heard a politician in an interview once say: "We go to church." The interviewer then asked, "Which church?" The politician then answered, "We like to keep our faith private, so don't worry about it." You might read that and say, "What a spineless Christian, if they're a Christian at all." Though we might make that accusation, how close does that hit to who we really are? Guys, let's face it; many of us have lost the commitment to take the gospel to our community.

Today, I want to remind you of the commission Jesus left us with in Matthew 28:19-20: *Go, therefore, and make disciples of all nations, baptizing them in the name of the Father and of the Son and of the Holy Spirit, teaching them to observe everything I have commanded you. And remember, I am with you always, to the end of the age.*

The gospel of Jesus Christ demands urgency! We need men who are committed to sharing the gospel, to making disciples. Being fully devoted followers of Christ is doing the common uncommonly well.

CONSISTENCY ————

1. Commit. Commit today to share the gospel with one person this week. Write down that person's name today as part of that commitment.

Name of person I will share the gospel with this week:

_____

2. Pray. Pray today that God will give you a heart for evangelism. Many people think they are not gifted in evangelism and use that as an excuse to not share the gospel. That excuse doesn't hold water. If you are a follower of Christ you are called to share.

3. Practice with a friend. This may sound cheesy, but it does help. If you're studying this book with a group, this will be easy. Divide into pairs and take turns sharing your faith with each other. Pretend as though the person you're talking to has never been to church and is not familiar with church lingo. Then share the gospel with them choosing your words wisely and explaining carefully.

DAY 6 MECHANICS OF DISCIPLESHIP

INTENSITY

The concept of discipleship is seen throughout the Bible. Moses poured into Joshua who would lead the Israelites into the promised land. Paul poured into Timothy and Titus who oversaw the early churches that Paul established. Jesus poured into 12 men who would lay the foundation for God's kingdom. All these disciple makers had one thing in common: they started a ministry that left a legacy.

I am confident that everyone desires to leave a legacy. The question we must ask ourselves is, what kind of legacy are we going to leave? After we are gone, the only legacy that will matter is our spiritual legacy. God does not measure success in this lifetime based on worldly accomplishments or riches. Instead, He will examine our obedience as believers and what we have accomplished for His kingdom.

Discipleship is not a suggestion. It is God's game plan for reaching the nations. As Paul said: *And what you have heard from me in the presence of many witnesses entrust to faithful men who will be able to teach others also* (2 Tim. 2:2, ESV). Jesus has entrusted every believer with the task of pouring into the next generation, and we have a choice. We will either choose to be an ambassador and mentor for the gospel, or we will spend our energy leaving a legacy for ourselves. Regardless of what we choose, God is going to complete His mission. We have to choose whether or not we will be a part of what He's doing.

Making disciples is no easy task. It demands sacrifice, patience, and love. Our lives will be open to scrutiny for those we lead. Remember that no one is perfect, but we are called to live holy lives. Regardless of your perceived knowledge, talents, or strengths, we all have something to give and something to learn when it comes to leading others. The goal of discipleship is twofold. The first is establishing and equipping young believers to make a difference for God's kingdom. The second is for us to become more like Christ. The end product is for both parties (mentor and mentee) to become more like Christ. However, this is impossible if we are not willing to accept the challenge and responsibility of leading others.

Day 1: Investment – Hebrews 10:24

1. Do you feel adequate to invest in others? If not, how do you tackle this insecurity so you can be used by God to the fullest?
2. How can you take time in a busy life to invest in others?
3. Who are you investing in?

Day 2: Balance – Romans 12:2

1. How hard is it for you to live a balanced lifestyle?
2. What are some simple ways you keep your life focused?
3. How do you keep from being conformed to this world?

Day 3: Influencers – Hebrews 12:14

1. Leadership is influence. Agree or disagree? Explain.
2. Are the leaders in your life more positional leaders or influential leaders? Explain.
3. What leadership characteristics are you reflecting?

Day 4: Accountability – Galatians 6:2

1. Why is accountability an important part of our spiritual lives?
2. Who holds you accountable?
3. What are some accountability questions you ask each other each time you meet?

Day 5: Commitment – Romans 9:3

1. How hard is it when you get around your realm of influence to remain committed to the things of Christ? Explain.
2. In what areas of life do you struggle to stay committed to Christ?
3. Are you committed to sharing the gospel? Explain. Who was last person you shared the gospel with?

MECHANICS OF THE BATTLE WITHIN

DAY 1 MECHANICS OF THE BATTLE WITHIN
FIGHTING RHABDOMYOLYSIS

If any of you lacks wisdom, let him ask God, who gives generously to all without reproach, and it will be given him. —James 1:5 (ESV)

"A rugby player performs intense sets of squat jumps on a hot day, collapses, and is rushed to the hospital, where he spends two days in intensive care. Doctors notice that his heart is beating abnormally and that he has unusually high levels of potassium in his blood. A soccer player runs a series of 100-meter sprints at near maximum intensity. After his eighth sprint he collapses to the ground; when he gets to the hospital he is found to have high levels of potassium and myoglobin in his bloodstream. He spends several days in the hospital and is unable to train for several weeks. A highly fit marathoner holds a 6:30 pace for 26 miles but collapses only a few feet short of the finish line. Blood tests reveal a potassium concentration three or four times the normal level and he dies."[18]

These athletes suffered from rhabdomyolysis, a condition caused by intense athletic activity.

Each of these athletes had a dream and they were going to do whatever it took to achieve that goal. They trained, pushed themselves, and never quit. What they did was not wrong. This article goes on to say: "one of the three CrossFit pillars (functionality, intensity, and variance) done, in extremis, can introduce a character to the scene whom we have dubbed 'Uncle Rhabdo.' Uncle Rhabdo is a close relative of 'Pukie' the vomiting clown. While Pukie represents a light hearted approach to the discomforts of training with intensity, his uncle depicts the dark, potentially deadly results of the inappropriate use of intensity." Intensity is a good thing until used unwisely. When you have no wisdom in your intensity, you are in a very dangerous situation.

The same happens to us with the battle within. When we lose the inward wisdom, we fall for the outward temptations. The outward temptations will bring us down the same way rhabdomyolysis brings down great athletes. Andy Stanley's book *The Best Question Ever* says that the best question ever is not *what is the right thing to do?* but, *what is the wise thing to do?*

The rightness or wrongness seems to be up for grabs on several issues in our society. We sometimes make our decisions about those issues based on popular opinion. Or we might say, "The Bible says nothing about _____, so it must be okay." We need to be careful not to wrongly justify our behavior and fall to temptation. When it comes to the life of partying, dating, relationships, marriage, jobs, sports, or anything we do, we must make a decision based on biblical wisdom, not just on what might seem right in the moment.

Recently, I was asked by a teenager if it would be okay for him to go to parties if he did not drink any of the alcohol. My immediate response was, "Do you believe that is a wise decision?" It would be difficult to answer affirmatively to that question, especially considering you can impact the same students just as well by not going. Guys, today I want you to evaluate every area of your life, and pray, "Lord, grant me wisdom in _____ (fill in the blank)." James tells us: *If any of you lacks wisdom, let him ask God, who gives generously to all without reproach, and it will be given him* (Jas. 1:5, ESV).

CONSISTENCY ———

1. Evaluate your decision-making. When faced with tough decisions, are you in the habit of asking, what is the wise thing to do? Why is that a good question to ask? Are you justifying any wrong behavior because you're basing your decisions on popular opinion? Explain.

2. Pray. Spend time today asking God to fill you with His wisdom. Claim the promise of James 1:5: *If any of you lacks wisdom, let him ask God, who gives generously to all without reproach, and it will be given him.*

3. Value the Word. Much of the wisdom God is going to give you is found in His Word. Be a student of the Scriptures. Read it. Study it. Meditate on it. Memorize it.

DAY 2 MECHANICS OF THE BATTLE WITHIN
THE BATTLE OF THE DOUBLE TAKE

I made a covenant with my eyes not to look lustfully at a young woman. —Job 31:1 (NIV)

The saying is true that "99 percent of men struggle with lust and the other 1 percent are liars." All men struggle with this battle. It is natural to be attracted to a person of the opposite sex. But when that attraction moves to lustful thoughts and intentions, we have transferred into sin. Today's focus, however, will be specifically on the "double take."

Most guys know what a double take is and we all have our own personal accounts of how it has negatively affected us as believers. One of mine happened at the 2013 CrossFit Games. If you are unfamiliar with the atmosphere of the CrossFit Games, then imagine twenty thousand people packed into a stadium who all have a common interest of pursuing elite fitness. You would be foolish to think that there would not be a struggle of lust when surrounded by ten thousand beautiful women, most of whom have a desire to show off their commitment to fitness. It is always a challenge to keep your eyes pure in that setting. At the 2013 Games, Rich Froning and I were walking down the beach when I saw a very beautiful woman in a bathing suit. Similar to a bug being drawn to the light, my eyes were glued to what I was seeing. Before I noticed what was happening, I received a very firm backhand across my chest. At first I was confused by Rich's action, but he looked at me and said, "No double takes." My sarcastic remark was that I didn't double take. Rather, I chose to keep my eyes focused on this lady for an extremely long time. He responded, "Same thing." Honestly, I was surprised that I did not get backhanded again for my sarcasm.

Double takes can reveal our hearts. When a guy stares at a woman for an extended period of time, it's usually not because he's trying to assess her spiritual condition. Most times it means his thoughts are moving into a place that is not spiritually healthy.

One of the biggest battles guys will face concerns our lustful thoughts. This battle has only two conclusions. Either we will choose to control it, or we will allow it to control us. Too many men chose not to control their lust and it has caused incredible damage to their lives and their relationships. And in the eyes of God there is no separation between intentions and actions. His Word states that *"anyone who looks at a woman lustfully has already committed adultery with her in his heart"* (Matt. 5:28, NIV). Before you judge a fallen brother, remind yourself that you are only one bad choice away from being in the same situation. If our eyes linger too long, or our thoughts stray from pure thinking, we quickly wade into sin. And if we continue to wade in that water, our sinful thoughts turn into sinful actions. Then devastating consequences follow.

We need to remember that God hates sin and desires for us to live holy lives. That should be our goal also. That will be difficult to do if we are walking on the edge, getting as close to the line of sin without crossing it. Instead, we should strive to get as far away from sin as possible. That's why Paul said we should *"Flee from youthful passions, and pursue righteousness, faith, love, and peace, along with those who call on the Lord from a pure heart* (2 Tim. 2:22). It's impossible to pursue holiness and righteousness if we are living in the world of double takes, seeing how far we can go without sinning.

The battle with lust is a constant battle, whether you're a teenager, young single adult, or a man who's been married for several years. Here's the battle: *For the desires of the flesh are against the Spirit, and the desires of the Spirit are against the flesh, for these are opposed to each other, to keep you from doing the things you want to do* (Gal. 5:17, ESV). This is a lifelong fight, but with Christ, you can prevail. Will you ever have victory over lust? Absolutely, you can find victory through Christ. This will require a daily discipline of turning our hearts and minds to Him. Our prayer must be the following: *Turn my eyes from looking at worthless things; and give me life in your ways* (Ps. 119:37, ESV). Put your hope in Christ, and you will find victory!

⊗ CONSISTENCY ———

1. Find accountability. *Two are better than one, because they have a good reward for their toil. For if they fall, one will lift up his fellow. But woe to him who is alone when he falls and has not another to lift him up!* (Ecc. 4:9-10, ESV). I know that story with Rich and me may seem cheesy, but Rich was simply doing his job. He knows that I desire to pursue righteousness, and at that moment I needed a friendly reminder to not double take. Find someone who will hold you to a high standard and give them permission to call you out (or sometimes a firm backhand across the chest may work).

2. Remind yourself of God's view of sin. God takes sin seriously. So seriously that He sent His Son as a sacrifice to cleanse us from it. *For you are not a God who delights in wickedness; evil may not dwell with you* (Ps. 5:4, ESV).

3. Pray for forgiveness. When you sin, don't hide it or dwell on it. Confess it before God. Remember: *If we say we have no sin, we deceive ourselves, and the truth is not in us. If we confess our sins, he is faithful and just to forgive us our sins and to cleanse us from all unrighteousness* (1 John 1:8-9, ESV).

4. Set boundaries. Be intentional about your purity. Make firm commitments about what you're going to read, view, and listen to, and relay those commitments to your accountability partner. Post this verse in a spot where you'll see it often: *I made a covenant with my eyes not to look lustfully at a young woman* (Job 31:1, NIV).

Train your eyes, mind, and heart to focus on Christ.

DAY 3 MECHANICS OF THE BATTLE WITHIN
BATTLING OUR IDENTITY

The good person out of the good treasure of his heart produces good, and the evil person out of his evil treasure produces evil, for out of the abundance of the heart his mouth speaks. —Luke 6:45 (ESV)

Our identity is the very thing that defines us as individuals. For some, their identity consists of being a father, husband, dentist, student, or athlete. The easiest way for a person to define themselves is through the things they enjoy the most. If you find joy in your children, then you will probably define yourself as a father. If you find joy in sports, then you will define yourself as an athlete. If you are a successful person, then you will likely define yourself through your career. Whatever the case may be, everyone has an identity.

In the 2010 CrossFit Games, Rich Froning made a name for himself. He was going into the last workout with a commanding lead, and his dream of being the "fittest man on earth" was within his grasp. All he needed to do was climb a 20-foot rope one more time, and victory would be his. The only problem was that he had never learned how to climb a rope with his feet. Rich Froning finished in second place that year because of the rope. For many, they would have been content with second place. But not Rich. The reason was because his identity was rooted in the wrong thing. More than anything else, Rich wanted to define himself as the "fittest man on earth."

For the following months, Rich wrestled with the question, *who am I?* Up until this point in his life, he had put his hope in being an athlete. If you were to ask Rich that question, he would have said, "a CrossFit athlete." Rich wanted to be remembered as the greatest of all time, but his identity had become an idol and left him empty. It wasn't until he surrendered his life to Christ in the following months that he would understand how to put his identity in Christ instead of CrossFit.

The line between identity and idolatry is very thin. Tim Keller says, "An idol is anything more important to you than God, anything that absorbs your heart and imagination more than God, anything you seek to give you only what God can give."[19] He continues to explain that idols are often not bad things. Instead, idols are more often good things that we have made ultimate things. The most common form of idolatry can arise from our family, comfort, work, or success. The truth is that anything that we value more than God becomes an idol. Therefore, we must be very cautious not to take good things that God has placed in our lives and make them ultimate things. When that happens, we value the gift, more than the Giver. Paul addressed this in Romans: *They exchanged the truth about God for a lie and worshiped and served the creature rather than the Creator* (Rom. 1:25, ESV).

The key is putting our identity in Christ. If we fail to put our identity in Christ, idols will rise from different areas of our lives. The goal is not to find a new career or a new hobby. Instead, the key to mortifying idols in our lives is having a heart change. The kind of heart change that only God can give: *And I will give them one heart, and a new spirit I will put within them. I will remove the heart of stone from their flesh and give them a heart of flesh that they may walk in my statutes and keep my rules and obey them. And they shall be my people, and I will be their God* (Ezek. 11:19-20, ESV). Without this heart change our identities will be rooted in something other than God, and at some point in our lives, that identity will fail us. That is what the rope did to Rich in 2010.

Can I continue to do what I love and still put my identity in Christ? Absolutely! Fast-forward to 2014. If you were to now ask Rich Froning, *who are you?*, he would say that he is a loved child of God who is saved through Jesus' blood. Rich did manage to put his identity in Christ. In the process, he also managed to win the 2011, 2012, 2013, and 2014 CrossFit Games. Many may think that Rich wants to be remembered as the greatest CrossFitter of all time, but that is not the case. He simply wants people to know Jesus. His goal is that people would come to worship his Creator instead of some creation. He lives out this verse: *He must increase, but I must decrease* (John 3:30, ESV).

⊗ CONSISTENCY ———

1) Identity check. Who or what is your identity rooted in? Family? Friends? Career? Sports? Christ? One way to answer this question is to look at your calendar. Where do you spend the majority of your time?

2) Idol check. Are there any idols in your life? As we previously mentioned, "An idol is anything more important to you than God, anything that absorbs your heart and imagination more than God, anything you seek to give you only what God can give" (Tim Keller).

3) Pray and be accountable. Give God freedom to point out idols in your life. Ask Him to show you what your identity is based on, and seek to find your identity in Christ. Discuss this with the guys who are holding you accountable. Give them permission to speak into your life concerning your identity and the idols you may have constructed.

4) Read and reflect on the following passage.

For although they knew God, they did not honor him as God or give thanks to him, but they became futile in their thinking, and their foolish hearts were darkened. Claiming to be wise, they became fools, and exchanged the glory of the immortal God for images resembling mortal man and birds and animals and creeping things. Therefore God gave them up in the lusts of their hearts to impurity, to the dishonoring of their bodies among themselves, because they exchanged the truth about God for a lie and worshiped and served the creature rather than the Creator, who is blessed forever! Amen.
—Romans 1:21-25 (ESV)

DAY 4 MECHANICS OF THE BATTLE WITHIN
SETTING BOUNDARIES

Be alert and of sober mind. Your enemy the devil prowls around like a roaring lion looking for someone to devour. Resist him, standing firm in the faith, because you know that the family of believers throughout the world is undergoing the same kind of sufferings.
—1 Peter 5:8-9 (NIV)

A common truth to being fit is: "You can do all of the activity you want. You still cannot outwork a bad diet." Bad diets are the death of so many great workouts. Most guys love food and will consume large amounts throughout the day. All fitness experts will tell you, though, that you can work out and have the best CrossFit coach in the world, but if your diet has no boundaries, your body will reflect what you are putting into it. The key to a good diet is setting boundaries to what and how much you eat. However, food is tempting. There is nothing like that fast-food burger, maybe a little Taco Bell®, or even those chicken nuggets from Chick-fil-A®. It is all called temptation.

There are also temptations that keep us from remaining spiritually healthy. First Peter 5:8 tells us the Devil is prowling around wanting to devour us. Have we set up boundaries to protect ourselves? Constantly we hear of men who have cheated on their spouse, got addicted to pornography, become intoxicated with alcohol, lost their virginity, or fallen into the world of drugs.

What's one cause of falling into the Devil's trap? A lack of boundaries. Today I want to challenge you to set some boundaries.

The first boundary to set as a man is to **protect the time.** Make sure you are protecting some time each day to spend with God. I would encourage you to start your day with this time as Jesus did: *Very early in the morning, while it was still dark, Jesus got up, left the house and went off to a solitary place, where he prayed* (Mark 1:35).

Meeting with God first helps you keep your mind focused on Christ through the day. You set the tone for God to speak to you throughout the day concerning your decisions and behaviors. When you protect the time, all other boundaries seem easier to live by.

The second boundary is what we call **not even a hint.** Hear Paul's words: *But among you there must not be even a hint of sexual immorality, or of any kind of impurity, or of greed, because these are improper for God's holy people* (Eph. 5:3, NIV). When we operate with the "not even a hint" principle, we are quick to turn away from impure thoughts, lustful looks, or other tempting situations. We operate in such a way that our lives display holiness in all we do.

The third boundary is **don't be alone.** Men need accountability. Those who enter the battle alone are much more vulnerable to the enemy's attack. Those who walk through the battle together can hold each other up. A different aspect of this boundary concerns the opposite sex. If you're a young guy, be careful about being alone with a date or love interest. While your intentions may be honorable, temptation can come on quickly and strongly when you're alone with that significant other.

If you're a married guy going through this study, create the boundary to never be alone in a private place with a woman who is not your wife. You don't want to put yourself in a tempting situation, nor do you want to give the appearance of anything improper.

Fourthly, let's be challenged by the old principle of **garbage in, garbage out.** Paul called for us to have pure minds: *Finally, brothers and sisters, whatever is true, whatever is noble, whatever is right, whatever is pure, whatever is lovely, whatever is admirable—if anything is excellent or praiseworthy—think about such things* (Phil. 4:8, NIV). What you put in your brain and allow into your life matters. The music you listen to, the books you read, the movies you watch, the people you date, the friends you hang out with, who you follow on social media, what you set your eyes on—all of it matters.

A fifth boundary, or you could say a key component we need as men, is **community.** This passage reminds of our need for community: *Though one may be overpowered, two can defend themselves. A cord of three strands is not quickly broken* (Eccl. 4:12, NIV). Men need other men as close friends.

Godly men know their limits and set boundaries in their lives. Boundaries show a sign of godly manhood, not weakness. Men who know their weaknesses and set boundaries to keep them from falling into their weaknesses are always the strongest men.

✇ CONSISTENCY ———

1. Check current boundaries. Boundaries are not always a joy to have. We have to remember, though, that they are a must for us if we want to live the life God has called us to. Go back through the five boundaries we listed today and evaluate how you're doing at living inside these boundaries.

2. Set new boundaries. What temptations do you struggle with the most? What are the weak areas of your life? Where do you need more discipline? It's in these areas that you need to set strong, consistent boundaries.

3. Accountability. Make sure your accountability group knows the boundaries you have set. Give them freedom to get your attention when they see your life slipping outside the boundaries.

DAY 5 MECHANICS OF THE BATTLE WITHIN
BATTLING PASSIVITY

Be watchful, stand firm in the faith, act like men, be strong.
—1 Corinthians 16:13 (ESV)

One of the goals of this book is for boys to become men. What does that mean? In our current society, we battle passivity more than ever. It is becoming increasingly common for men to delay their calling to step up and accept responsibility.

According to a "This Is Money" article released in February 2012, the employment rate of men in 1952 was 96 percent. Fast-forward 60 years, and the employment rate of men is now 75 percent. What has changed? Men are failing to step up to the plate and fulfill their responsibilities as leaders and providers for their families. According to that same article, adults under the age of 25 in 1952 made up one-third of the working population. But now, that number has dropped to one-seventh. The people claiming unemployment has increased from 350,000 to 1.6 million in the last 60 years. So what is the big issue? Passivity![20]

Passivity can be contagious, negatively affecting multiple aspects of a guy's life. It has the potential to impact your academics, fitness, finances, job, and relationships. For young men, it causes you to shirk your responsibility to be the son, student, teammate, coworker, and friend you are supposed to be. For older guys, passivity creeps into your role as leader and provider. Your marriage, children, job, and church suffers.

One of the biggest reasons for passivity in our society is the expectations of parents and their children. It's common these days for young adults (ages 18-25) to still be dependent upon their parents. They often wait until after high school, college, or even landing their first "big boy" job before ever accepting responsibility for their needs or actions as young adults. This prolonged journey of putting off responsibility has stunted the growth of maturity in our young adults. But, who is to blame?

Some may look at this dilemma and place all the blame on the parents. While others give the parents a pass and say the blame is on the child. Usually the truth is somewhere in the middle.

Regardless of your age, you can begin to accept responsibility and start the journey of biblical manhood. The first step is by striving for self-dependency.

Please don't misunderstand. It is not realistic for a 14-year-old boy in our society to completely leave the dependency of his parents. Nor should parents kick their teenage son out on the street. However, there should be an atmosphere of responsibility and maturity for all ages.

All guys should be learning how to become self-sufficient on the road to being fully independent. To put that into perspective, no one drops a toddler off the deep end of a pool without giving him swim lessons first. As a young guy, you may not be ready to fully provide for yourself, but you can began to accept responsibility by working part time, doing chores around the house, paying for gas, making car payments or paying car insurance, and so on. The transition from boy to biblical manhood does not happen overnight. Therefore, there needs to be a continual effort from both you and your parents to fight against passivity.

Paul rebuked the Corinthians about their immaturity: *I fed you with milk, not solid food, for you were not ready for it. And even now you are not yet ready* (1 Cor. 3:2, ESV). Part of becoming biblical men and fighting passivity is growing spiritually. When we first come into a relationship with Christ, we are learning just the basics of the faith. Much of that time we are dependent on others to teach us God's Word. In fact, there will never be a time in our lives as believers that we will not need community and accountability in our lives. But, as we grow, we need to take on more difficult, deeper issues of the faith. And we should reach a point where we are not totally dependent on others to should reach a point where we are not totally dependent on others to teach us. We need to be learning through our quiet time and personal study. We need to make a daily decision to accept responsibility for growing in our faith. That will be the only way we can become biblical men. It is not a process that will happen overnight. But we must take responsibility and be committed to the journey.

⊗ CONSISTENCY ———

1) Fight passivity by valuing God's Word. It will be impossible to become the biblical man God has called you to be if you are not spending quality time investing in God's Word. Biblical men separate themselves from the world by transforming their thoughts and pursuits in life. Learn to separate yourself as a biblical man by renewing your mind daily through God's Word. As Paul urged us: *Do not be conformed to this world, but be transformed by the renewal of your mind, that by testing you may discern what is the will of God, what is good and acceptable and perfect* (Rom. 12:2, ESV).

2) Fight passivity by growing as a provider. One of the biggest responsibilities you will take on at some point in life is as provider. As a young man, the responsibility to provide for your family probably doesn't rest on you. But what are some character qualities you can begin to cultivate to prepare you for that responsibility? One thing to do is develop a servant's heart. A godly man no longer views his marriage, finances, and career as an opportunity to serve himself. Instead, his focus is to lead his family, provide for his family, and use his resources for God.

3) Fighting passivity starts by forming good habits. Maybe it is accepting some type of financial responsibility, committing to some type of Scripture memory, or making a healthy decision to eat cleaner or work out consistently. Stop making excuses and form habits that help you fight passivity.

DAY 6 MECHANICS OF THE BATTLE WITHIN
INTENSITY

A guy's greatest battles happen on the inside. Every day we have inward decisions to make that will reflect what happens on the outside. We have an inner drive that pushes and pulls us. Every day we battle the temptations of the world to live godly, pure lives. Many guys are losing this battle. Too many are addicted to pornography, following people on social media who post inappropriate pictures, or watching inappropriate and unholy movies and TV shows. Godly men are falling every day. This has to change.

This week we were challenged to live differently by setting boundaries, not doing the double take, not falling for the lust of influence, and not being passive. But as with a fitness workout, what good is it if we aren't consistent so that we become stronger and more in shape? One week is not going to make that much of a difference. Reading about "the battle within" one week and not making a change to your lifestyle means nothing. Psalm 42:1 says: *As the deer pants for streams of water, so my soul pants for you, O God* (NIV). When we long for the things of God more than we long for the lust of our flesh, we will change.

What are you going to do with the challenges from this week? Nathan Wagnon and Brian Mills wrote in *Checkpoints: A Tactical Guide to Manhood*, "The discipline of self-control is absolutely essential to becoming a man of God. If we do not learn to control the self, we naturally drift toward 'sexual immorality, impurity and debauchery; idolatry and witchcraft; hatred, discord, jealousy, fits of rage, selfish ambition, dissensions, factions and envy; drunkenness, orgies' and stuff like that (Gal. 5:19-21)."[21]

Day 1: Fighting Rhabdomyolysis – James 1:5

1. Are you living your life with spiritual wisdom? What is the evidence?
2. How does temptation pull you away from spiritual disciplines?
3. What is the greatest temptation you face and what are you doing to keep from falling into it?

Day 2: The Battle of the Double Take – Job 31:1

1. How hard is it to not go back for a double take?
2. Who in your life can ask you the tough questions when it comes to temptations?
3. Quote Job 31:1 without looking.

Day 3: Battling Our Identity – Luke 6:45

1. What social media site provides the greatest temptation for you? What are you doing about it?
2. What barriers have you put on your phone/computer to help protect you from temptation?
3. Have you seen a pornographic image online? Have you blocked that site? Have you run from that temptation? Explain.

Day 4: Setting Boundaries – 1 Peter 5:8-9

1. What does it mean to set boundaries in our lives? Why is it so important that we set appropriate ones?
2. Out of all the boundaries we read about on this day, which one hit home with you the most and why?
3. In what area of your life do you need to set up boundaries today?

Day 5: Battling Passivity – 1 Corinthians 16:13

1. How do you see the battle of passivity happening around you?
2. What areas of responsibility are pushing you toward manhood?
3. What habits in your life challenge you to fight against passivity?

MECHANICS OF RELATIONSHIPS

DAY I MECHANICS OF RELATIONSHIPS
AUTHORITY

Do not rebuke an older man harshly, but exhort him as if he were your father. Treat younger men as brothers, older women as mothers, and younger women as sisters, with absolute purity.
—1 Timothy 5:1-2 (NIV)

"Respect your elders" seems to be a phrase of the past. The new phrase seems to be "I will respect those who deserve my respect." This is contrary to what the Bible teaches.

If you read the book of Ephesians, you will find these commands: "Children obey your parents"; "Honor your Father and mother"; "Fathers do not exasperate your children"; "Slaves obey your earthly master." What you do not find is this: "Obey and honor only if the authority in your life is worthy of obeying and honoring." Ephesians 6:7-8 says: *Serve wholeheartedly, as if you were serving the Lord, not people, because you know that the Lord will reward each one for whatever good they do, whether they are slave or free* (NIV). We are to honor the authorities in our lives even when they are not honorable. I've seen many teenagers walk away from a workout because they did not like how the coach was treating them. I've seen teens yell and fight with their parents because they say, "My parents just don't understand." We have to remember that our circumstances and mood do not change who is in authority over our lives.

Sometimes this generation growing up today is called the entitled generation. Many young men think they deserve more than they are given. If they are not given what they want, they quit. If they are not respected, they will not give respect. If they are not honored, they will never give honor. They give little or no respect to the authorities in their lives. As a godly young man, you need to rise above this. You need to understand that God has placed authorities in your life for your good and His purpose.

The only time disobedience is allowed is when you are asked to do something immoral, illegal, or harmful to yourself or others. And there may be times when you must disobey authorities in order to further the gospel, as the apostles faced in Acts 4. However, most of us don't live under those conditions at this time. Be sure this kind of disobedience is Holy Spirit-led. One note: if your parents have grounded you from church, this is not an opportunity to disobey them. The unchurched who are in authority over us stand a stronger chance of coming to Christ through our obedience than through our disobedience.

Jackie Robinson illustrates this principle. Jackie was the first African American man to ever get the chance to play in Major League Baseball. The movie *42* (Warner Bros., 2013) is based on the true story of Jackie's rise in baseball. There is a scene where Branch Rickey, the owner of the Dodgers, is talking to Jackie about placing him on the team. By doing so, Jackie would be the first African American man in the majors. Jackie asks Rickey if he wants a player who has the guts to fight back at the critics. Branch Rickey says, "No, I want a player who's got the guts not to fight back." He was letting Jackie know that he needed a man who could submit to some of the most disrespectable authority during that time. Jackie Robinson did that very thing. His obedience led to huge changes in Major League Baseball.

We need young men willing to honor the authorities God has placed over them.

 CONSISTENCY ———

1. Pray for authorities. Probably most of us have authorities that we struggle with. Instead of complaining about them, take time to pray for them. Pray about how you can honor them and show Christ's love to them.

2. Ask for forgiveness. I am going to challenge the little boy in you to sit down and the man in you to stand up. You need to go to the people you have dishonored and ask for their forgiveness. You need to let them know that your behavior has not been the behavior of a fully devoted follower of Christ.

3. Reread Ephesians 6:1-8 and 1 Timothy 5:1-2. List the key words and phrases. Meditate on the words of these passages and pray about how you need to implement these truths into your life.

DAY 2 MECHANICS OF RELATIONSHIPS
RESPECT

Servants, be subject to your masters with all respect, not only to the good and gentle but also to the unjust. —1 Peter 2:18 (ESV)

Respect is admiration for someone based on their abilities, qualities, and achievements. Does that mean that someone who does not possess admirable talents and achievements does not earn our respect? Absolutely not. Respect is a foundational pillar for good relationships. If you want to have a healthy relationship with your parents, a boss, or a coach, then you must show respect. Does that mean that the only people you should strive to show respect to are those in an authoritative role in your life? Not at all. We should strive to be respectful to our friends, our teammates, and our coworkers. If you desire respect from others, then you must first learn how to respect others.

Where does respect begin? Respect begins with humility. The first chapter of this book describes the mechanics of humility and how it is essential for the spiritual life of a believer. It is difficult to respect others if you have a prideful view of yourself.

Humility and respect are inseparable. If you demand others to think highly of you, then they will begin to lose respect for you. The opposite effect can also hold true. If you begin to respect others, they will recognize your humility and think highly of you. The best example of humility is Jesus: *Have this mind among yourselves, which is yours in Christ Jesus, who, though he was in the form of God, did not count equality with God a thing to be grasped, but emptied himself, by taking the form of a servant, being born in the likeness of men. And being found in human form, he humbled himself by becoming obedient to the point of death, even death on a cross. Therefore God has highly exalted him and bestowed on him the name that is above every name, so that at the name of Jesus every knee should bow, in heaven and on earth and under the earth, and every tongue confess that Jesus Christ is Lord, to the glory of God the Father* (Phil. 2:5-11, ESV).

There is no better picture of a balance of humility and respect than these seven verses. Jesus was/is equal with God, but He humbled Himself by taking on the form of man (who He created) and suffering the worst possible death. This is the good news of the gospel. If Jesus would have thought too highly of Himself, then there would be no gospel and we would have no Savior. However, Jesus humbled Himself and chose to abandon His rightful place on the throne as the Creator of the universe. Then, throughout His ministry, He showed respect to others, putting their needs before His own. Ultimately, He took the sin of humanity upon Himself and died the sacrificial death on the cross: *For our sake he made him to be sin that knew no sin, so that in him we might become the righteousness of God* (2 Cor. 5:21, ESV).

After this perfect act of humility and respect, He was restored to His rightful place on the throne. Jesus will be forever exalted for His perfect sacrifice. The beauty of the gospel is that Jesus showed us how humility and respect are inseparable. We do not have to guess about how we can make a difference in this lifetime. Instead, we only need to turn to Jesus' example and follow His lead. Many great people have achieved great things in their lives, but no name echoes louder in human history than Jesus. Napoleon, a powerful and highly respected man, had this to say about Jesus: "I know men; and I tell you that Jesus Christ is no mere man. Between Him and every person in the world there is no possible term of comparison. Alexander, Caesar, Charlemagne, and I have founded empires. But on what did we rest the creations of our genius? Upon force. Jesus Christ founded His Empire upon love; and at this hour millions of men would die for him."[22]

No one will ever display a better example of love for others rooted in the balance of humility and respect than Jesus. The gospel still has the world's most powerful and successful men flabbergasted at what Jesus accomplished and how He did it.

What does this mean for us as believers? This means that no matter how successful, rich, or powerful you may become in this lifetime, you will never compare to Jesus and His perfect act of love. We must strive to take on the mentality of Paul, who said: *But far be it from me to boast except in the cross of our Lord Jesus Christ, by which the world has been crucified to me, and I to the world* (Gal. 6:14, ESV). That is why the world's best CrossFit athlete, Rich Froning, wears it on his side. Rich has understood that all of his achievements will fall infinitely short of the one great achievement, the gospel.

When it comes down to it, none of us have anything to boast about. We have nothing except what we have in Jesus. Let's follow His example of humility and respect.

⊗ CONSISTENCY ———

1) Study the Word. Spend time today studying Philippians 2:5-11. Reflect on these verses and ask yourself how you can follow Jesus' example of humility and respect. Whether it is your parents, siblings, boss, or someone you have a hard time loving, you should strive to show respect to all.

2) Humble yourself. If you want to gain the respect of others, then you must first have a humble view of yourself. Don't seek out respect from others. Instead, seek to serve others and put their needs before your own, and you will begin to earn the respect of others around you. We must first know how to serve and respect others before we can gain respect. Live this passage out: *Do nothing from selfish ambition or conceit, but in humility count others more significant than yourselves. Let each of you look not only to his own interests, but also to the interests of others* (Phil. 2:3-4, ESV).

DAY 3 MECHANICS OF RELATIONSHIPS
HONESTY

Whoever walks in integrity walks securely, but whoever takes crooked paths will be found out. —Proverbs 10:9 (NIV)

Do you remember the story of the boy who cried wolf? He was a shepherd boy who was bored. To amuse himself, he cried out, "Wolf! Wolf! A wolf is chasing the sheep!" When the villagers heard his cry, they came running, but all they found was a little shepherd boy laughing. He did this again, and again the villagers came to his rescue only to find him laughing. When he actually saw a real wolf, he let out a cry, but none of the villagers came. Later that evening, the villagers came to the hilltop to find no sheep and a crying shepherd boy. When asked what happened, he told them. Then one older, wiser man told the boy, "Nobody believes a liar...even when he is telling the truth!"

Integrity is a characteristic that has been lost in today's men. Many guys lie, cheat, or do whatever it takes to get what they want. We see this in sports all the time. How many professional and college athletes are getting suspended due to cheating? Guys sacrifice their integrity to impress their coaches, teachers, girlfriends, parents, and others to get something they want.

For guys, maintaining their integrity is a constant battle that can be lost in a moment. One wrong choice, one slip-up, can destroy what a guy has worked long and hard to establish.

The first step in being a man of integrity is being in the Word daily. When we wake up in the morning and spend a few minutes with the Lord, we have a greater chance of thinking like Christ throughout the day. You become like the people you hang out with and if you spend time with Christ daily you will act like Christ daily.

The second step to being a man of integrity is surrounding yourself with men of integrity. Those who hang out with cheaters and liars become cheaters and liars. Have you ever worked out with someone who cheats on their workouts? I remember a boy from our high school basketball team who would skip parts of his workout every time the coach turned his back. How does that make you better? How do you think his work ethic affected his teammates? Typically, if you continue to work out with someone who shortens their reps, turns off the video early, cuts the corner, runs a little slower, or even quits halfway through if no one is looking, then you will do the same. If your workout partner cheats, then you cheat. It is the same in life. If the ones you spend the most time with are not men of integrity, you will not be either.

A third step in working toward being a man of integrity is acting with godly wisdom. Opportunities always have consequences. Some good, some bad. However, many men throw their reputation out the window because they choose wrongly when an opportunity arises. Over the years, I have watched guys who were well-respected for their faith and integrity end up with opposite reputations because of their wrong choices.

One of the best illustrations of sacrificing integrity came in the 1988 summer Olympics®. The 100-meter sprint was the highlight of the Olympics, and thousands of people came to watch the race between Ben Johnson of Canada and Carl Lewis of the United States. Carl Lewis was the defending gold medalist of the previous summer Olympics and Ben Johnson was the current world champion with the current world record. With everyone watching the final race, Ben dominated the field with a time of 9.79 seconds. This was a new world record, crushing Carl's time of 9.92 seconds. Carl's time was good enough for a U.S. record and a silver medal. Later, however, the integrity of Ben Johnson would be revealed. It was determined through drug testing that he had cheated and was using steroids at the time of his performance. Not only would Ben's integrity pay the price, but he was stripped of his gold medal. The gold medal was awarded to Carl Lewis for his ability to perform at the highest level within the rules that were established by the Olympic committee.

Honesty is lacking in many men today. Our integrity is under attack with the pressures of life. We must wake up every day committed to living a life that represents Christ even if it is not the popular or cool thing to do. No matter the cost, we must be men of Integrity.

✪ CONSISTENCY ————

1. Stay true no matter what. For years, integrity has been defined as "who you are when no one else is looking." When you are online, do you stay true to who you are and who God has made you, or do you cave to the temptations that come your way?

2. Don't take shortcuts. Shortcuts do not build champions. Champions are made in the grind. Rich Froning would not be a four-time CrossFit winner if he cheated on his workouts or in the games. Where in your life are you cheating and how can you change? Most men would never cheat on their workouts or in their social lives, but in their spiritual life they take shortcuts every day. How are you doing in your spiritual life? Are you cheating God with your time? How can you adjust your time so that you are not cheating God?

3. Commit to be a man of integrity. We need men who are willing to be honest no matter what. You are growing up in a culture that says it's OK to lie and cheat to get what you want. Don't fall for that lie. Honor God by doing things the right way. Live with integrity.

DAY 4 MECHANICS OF RELATIONSHIPS
COMMUNICATION

Know this, my beloved brothers: let every person be quick to hear, slow to speak, slow to anger; for the anger of man does not produce the righteousness of God. —James 1:19-20 (ESV)

We live in a world today that is fast to speak, slow to listen, and quick to become angry.

I was at a dodgeball tournament once where the winning team won eight hundred dollars cash. As the tournament came down to the last few teams, the competitive spirit was coming out strong. During the semifinals, one particular team (the team that was winning) started talking a little trash. As you might imagine, this caused a great deal of frustration among the opposing team. When the trash-talking team won, the losing team followed them off the court and a fight ensued. The fight was a result of poor communication that led to anger. "The only way that peace can prevail with the 'everyone' to whom the admonitions apply is to be ready listeners and slow commentators, especially in heated situations."[23]

James 1:19-20 speaks to the life of every man in three ways. First, we must be quick to hear. Let's be honest—most of us are slow to hear. We would rather argue or fight than listen. This probably happens in your relationships with parents, teammates, and friends. Listening first helps you be slow to speak. Then, as you practice a cautious response to people, it is amazing how quickly angry emotions inside yourself and from others will die.

Men seem to let everything get to them. We can't even drive down the road without getting mad. We let people upset us at school, in the locker rooms, and in our homes. Yet if we pause in our anger and listen, we will become less agitated and more understanding.

If we gain these three characteristics listed in James, we will become a more influential leader who has the chance to make a great impact for Christ. "The command to be quick to listen calls for an eagerness to hear and obey God's message. The appeal to be slow to speak demands silence until we have understood and applied the message. It is a call for restraint lest we produce hasty, ill-timed reactions. The challenge to be slow to become angry warns against hostile, bitter feelings. We cannot hear God if we remain distracted with resentment, hatred, or vengeful attitudes."[24]

As we wrap up this devotion, apply the teaching to your relationship with God. How do you respond to Him? Are you quick to listen or quick to speak? Are you quick to get angry or quick to let the peace of God come over you? Are you willing to hear from God or do you just talk to Him the whole time? A lot of times our relationship with God seems to be one-sided. We speak and we expect Him to listen, and we get mad when we don't get our way.

Today, practice the command from James—quick to hear, slow to speak, slow to get angry—in every relationship.

✪ CONSISTENCY ————

1. Be quick to listen Look back over the past few days in your relationships with your parents, friends, and God. Were you quick to listen? Or did you jump in with your agenda? Commit to listen first.

2. Be slow to speak. If you struggle with this, you might hear this phrase from those closest to you: "If you will just be quiet you will get in less trouble and cause less problems." This is me. I have been told this my whole life. Don't excuse the behavior by saying that's just who you are. It's a character flaw. Take it to the Lord and allow Him, by His Spirit, to change you.

3. Be slow to get angry. Do you have a quick temper? Does road rage rise in you in a hurry? Can you have a conversation or play a sport without getting mad? I know many men who are quick to anger and I know few people who love hanging out with them. Those who are quick to anger lose influence faster than anyone else.

Do you need to have a spiritual attitude adjustment today? Receive this passage and understand what God is saying to you. Repent of your anger and allow God to change it. This may take time.

One idea on how to control your temper is to memorize Scripture about anger, then meditate on it. Allow God's Word to change you. Also, talk to your accountability group about how you want to change. Allow them to hold you accountable and don't get angry when they do.

DAY 5 MECHANICS OF RELATIONSHIPS
LOYALTY

Never let loyalty and faithfulness leave you. Tie them around your neck; write them on the tablet of your heart. Then you will find favor and high regard in the sight of God and man. —Proverbs 3:3-4

Loyalty is a desired attribute that is rarely found in our fast-paced society. People are consumed by the next best thing. Whether it is cell phones, Internet connection, or social media, everyone wants the latest and greatest. Once they find it, very few stay loyal to their current device or contract. They jump in a hurry. My fear is that this mindset is trickling into our relationships.

In a society where everything revolves around "me, myself, and I," there's not much loyalty to be found.

Think about it. If I want food, then I drive around a building and pick it up. If I want to know the answer to a problem, then I look it up instantly on my phone. If I want to get coffee, then I drive to one of the many coffee shops in my city and order it. It's quick and simple. However, relationships are not that easy. And being loyal to others requires a lot of effort.

Loyalty demands sacrifice and inconvenience. It can become burdensome to those who are centered on themselves. If our primary focus is our needs, our agendas, and our desires, then loyalty just gets in the way. And similar to getting food, checking the phone, and grabbing coffee, we are hard-wired to run at the first sign of issues. What happens when there is a line to pick up food or coffee? We leave. My fear is that we treat our relationships the same way.

One of the best sources I have found on this topic is the book *Relationships: A Mess Worth Making* by Paul Tripp and Timothy Lane. They discuss how relationships are very difficult and challenging, and only those who are committed to each other will survive them.

Whether it involves family, friendships, or teammates, it is important to know that you are creating either good or bad habits. Every day you have the decision to give up on others or choose to work it out. Based on the high divorce rate inside and outside the church, we know many choose the easy way out. Giving up on others should always be a last resort. Think about it. What if we trained ourselves to never give up?

One of the greatest lessons CrossFit has taught me is to never give up. Even when the workout is extremely tough and I feel like I cannot do one more rep, something inside of me tells me to keep going. Relationships should be treated the same. No matter the difficulty of our situation or relationship, remember that you always have a choice to either quit or keep on fighting through it.

If I look at a workout and it looks comfortable and not challenging, then I probably am not getting fitter by doing it. On the other hand, if I look at a workout and think, I don't know how I am going to do this, it is often the very thing I need to do to get better. Relationships work in the same manner. It is often when I am faced with conflict or a situation that I don't know how to handle that my character and loyalty are tested. It is easy to respond in a loving way to others when things are going smoothly. It is difficult, however, to respond in a Christ-centered way to others when things are not working out the way we thought. We may look dazed and confused in a difficult conflict, but if we choose to commit and keep fighting, things often smooth out and we are glad we didn't give up.

Keep in mind that if we have received Christ, He lives in us. His love is in us. 1 John 4:19 says: *We love because He first loved us.* Because His love is in us we can love others, even through the difficult times. We can be more accepting, more forgiving, and more patient because His Spirit is working through us. That will help us not give up when we face difficult times in our relationships.

Every CrossFitter has thought about quitting at some point in a workout. There is often a point in a workout where a CrossFitter will ask themselves, *Is this really worth it?* The answer to that question and our relationships is YES! It is absolutely worth it! And it is also important to know that you are not the only one facing that difficult workout or circumstance. There is no controversy that you are currently facing in your relationships that someone has not already faced. Many people have been in the exact same position as you, and they too had one of two decisions—to quit or keep going. How you answer that question will often reveal the extent of your loyalty to others.

Many in our world lay loyalty to the side at the first sign of trouble in their relationships. Virtuosity calls for a young man to live differently.

 CONSISTENCY ———

1) Don't quit. If you're in a relationship that's struggling, don't quit. Give your best in that relationship and love with the love of Jesus. Embrace Paul's words: *Be completely humble and gentle; be patient, bearing with one another in love* (Eph. 4:2, NIV).

This will not be easy, but it is the standard that God has called us to in our relationships with others.

2) Talk with God. When you're faced with difficult relationship situations, first lay your burdens before the Lord and learn from His Word. Give Him freedom to direct your relationships.

3. Get godly counsel. Lean on godly mentors and friends who have walked the same path you're walking. Sometimes the best lessons are the ones you do not have to learn the hard way. Learn from others' mistakes, and strive to make your relationships better by avoiding some unnecessary pains. Hear this truth from Proverbs: *Whoever trusts in his own mind is a fool, but he who walks in wisdom will be delivered* (Prov. 28:26, ESV).

DAY 6 MECHANICS OF RELATIONSHIPS

INTENSITY

Regardless of the stage in life, relationships seem to be one of our greatest challenges.

Think of how the Israelites felt at the end of Moses' leadership. Due to an act of disobedience, he was unable to enter the land of Canaan (Num. 20:1-13). Moses knew it was time to step down and turn over leadership. That brings us to a powerful moment in Deuteronomy 31:6: *Be strong and courageous. Do not be afraid or terrified because of them, for the LORD your God goes with you; he will never leave you nor forsake you.*

Moses had said several times, including here: *The LORD your God.* He wanted them to know that their faith was not dependent on him. "God's program for the nation did not depend on any one human leader. It depended only on God's power to fulfill His own covenantal promises."[25]

Before a response is ever given, we must remember that "the Lord our God" is the One in charge of us. We should respond in all circumstances with holiness and faith. Is that how we respond? As you read on through the transition of Moses to Joshua, the people often responded to the commands of God with disobedience and frustration.

Today, we need men who are going to hear the call of God in their lives and respond with great faith and trust. Unfortunately, many guys have a rebellious attitude. The rebellious heart must become the obedient heart so that God can use you to impact the world.

Is God in charge of your relationships? Do you respond to the authorities in your life with godliness? Are you a man of great respect even when respect is not deserved? Is honesty a valued aspect of your character? What comes out of our mouths in communication? Is it an attitude of holiness? Are you loyal to the things of God and to the relationships in your life? Relationships are taking a hit today by the enemy, and we need men of God to step up and start leading according to His purpose and character.

Day 1: Authority – 1 Timothy 5:1-2.

1. In today's culture, what is the level of respect for authority?
2. How would you define the phrase "entitled generation"? Do you see this being a problem in our society today? Explain.
3. What will you do to better respect the authorities in your life?

Day 2: Respect – 1 Peter 2:18

1. How would you define respect?
2. How important is respect to relationships? How have you seen respect make a difference in a relationship?
3. What is your biggest barrier to being a man of respect?

Day 3: Honesty – Proverbs 10:9

1. Are the guys around you men of integrity? Explain.
2. Why do you think it is hard, at times, to have integrity?
3. Who is your model for a life of integrity? What are you learning from him?

Day 4: Communication – James 1:19-20

1. Do you find people today to be good or bad communicators? Explain.
2. What do you think is hurting our ability to communicate?
3. What are some simple principles that can help you communicate with respect and honor in your relationships?

Day 5: Loyalty – Proverbs 3:3-4

1. Where do you see a lack of loyalty the most? What is the cause of this problem?
2. How would you assess your loyalty in relationships?
3. What can we do as men to be more loyal to those around us?

MECHANICS OF ATTITUDE

DAY 1 MECHANICS OF ATTITUDE
MOTIVATION

*And whatever you do, in word or deed, do everything in the name of
the Lord Jesus, giving thanks to God the Father through him.*
—*Colossians 3:17 (ESV)*

Motivation is the desire to do something. It comes and goes very
quickly. We have all experienced days we were either extremely
productive or lazy. Motivation is the independent variable that drives
successful people. It is practically impossible to achieve great things
without being motivated by something or someone.

Motivation is a means to an end. Motivation without application
often results in lost opportunity. We must learn how to find a consistent
state of motivation and how to capitalize on it. In doing so, the first
question we must ask ourselves is, who or what is motivating us? If
we are being motivated by temporary things, then our motivation will
only be temporary. Money, success, and approval of others will only
motivate us for so long. At some point, there is not enough money or
praise of others that can keep us going.

There are many examples of successful people who achieved great
things in life. Whether it is winning championships, inventing some new
version of technology, or running a Fortune 500 company, motivation
is essential to finding success in life. But does that success bring joy?
A person can achieve great things and then ask themselves, *Is there
more to life than this?* How many superstars have been the best at their
sport, risen to the top, and won multiple championships, but were
still unsatisfied? One of the most telling interviews I have seen on this
is Tom Brady's *60 Minutes* interview. If you are unfamiliar with Tom
Brady, he is regarded as one of the best football players of all time.
He also is a multimillionaire who is married to a model. Most would
be envious of this life. Yet, he said in his interview that he still felt like

something was missing. Tom is a great example of how someone can be extremely motivated and achieve great success. However, without true fulfillment, motivation can only get you so far.

Instead, we must be inspired by something eternal and of infinite value. This is the only way we can find a consistent state of motivation and true joy. We must change our focus: *If then you have been raised with Christ, seek the things that are above, where Christ is, seated at the right hand of God. Set your minds on things that are above, not on things that are on earth* (Col. 3:1-2, ESV). Learn to look at things with an eternal perspective instead of a temporary one. When we look at life and our opportunities in light of the gospel, it makes everything clear. We understand exactly what we are called to do and how we are called to do it. This allows us to be motivated by what matters, and ultimately gives our life meaning and purpose.

No doubt certain men will be remembered throughout history by what they accomplished. But what do you want to be remembered for? You can use worldly motivation to make much of your own name, or you can use eternal motivation found only in the gospel to make much of Christ's name. Whichever path you choose to follow will likely determine the amount of joy you find in this lifetime.

Think of motivation as similar to money, success, or relationships. All of these things can be used in a God-glorifying way, or they can all be used in a self-promoting way.

✪ CONSISTENCY ────

1) Find right motivation. Embrace this promise: *Delight yourself in the LORD, and he will give you the desires of your heart* (Ps. 37:4, ESV).

Who are you seeking to delight? Yourself? Someone else? Or the Lord? When your motivation is to please the Lord, you may not achieve worldly fame or success, but you will make a real difference that lasts into eternity.

2) Desire to leave a godly legacy. Legacy makers are those who are motivated by the gospel, and driven by a passion to be used by God. Men do not leave a godly legacy by accident. They are intentional with their time and strive to make the most of every opportunity God has given them. They understand their purpose in life and want to inspire others to follow Christ. So, you should, *look carefully then how you walk, not as unwise but as wise, making the best use of the time, because the days are evil* (Eph. 5:15-16, ESV). And live such a life that you can say with Paul: *Be imitators of me, as I am of Christ* (1 Cor. 11:1, ESV).

DAY 2 MECHANICS OF ATTITUDE
HARD WORK

Whatever you do, work at it with all your heart, as working for the Lord, not for human masters. —Colossians 3:23 (NIV)

You can only go as high as your attitude takes you. The depth and consistency of your walk with Christ will often be determined by your attitude.

Frustration will happen. Difficulties will arise. Questions will surface. Doubt will linger. And life will get hard. But the one who remains committed to their walk with Christ will have a greater understanding of the circumstances life throws at them. Their attitude of endurance will see them through to the end.

An athlete's attitude will determine if they will ever be referred to as a champion. Shortcuts don't build champions, only hard work does. I watch so many men give up when times get hard. It might be in a workout, in a relationship, on a team, or with family, but men seem to be giving up when the work piles on.

The Bible speaks clearly about not giving up, about persevering. The greatest example is Jesus. Despite the difficulties, Jesus remained faithful and committed to His purpose.

When Paul wrote Colossians 3:23 he wanted to change the condition of the work ethic of slavery by challenge them from within. His words are clear: *Whatever you do, work at it with all your heart, as working for the Lord, not for human masters* (NIV).

Notice the phrase, "with all your heart." Many guys today love to take shortcuts. You find a girl who always has her homework done and you cheat off of her. You do "just enough" in your job so your boss does not get mad at you. Instead of completing the whole workout, you just go until you're tired, then you take shortcuts just to get through it. We live in a world of those who take shortcuts in their everyday lives, as well as in their spiritual lives. Where are the men who are all in? The "100 percenters"?

When men are committed to their walk with Christ with all their heart, they are less likely to fall into the quitter's mentality.

Paul said they should work "as for the Lord." Keep in mind who you're really working for. When the job gets tough or the assignment gets long, keep at it with the Lord in mind. Your hard work honors Him. Don't work to please your boss or your teacher, work to please the One who created you and saved you. If you do that, you'll honor both your boss and teacher.

Also, it's easy to get lost working for our own fame and success. Remember you're not here to further your kingdom, you're here to further Christ's. God has placed you on this planet and given you talent to use to make Him famous. Who are you working for?

Endure. Persevere. Work hard...for the right One.

✪ CONSISTENCY ━━━

1. Work with all your heart. Check your work ethic. Would those around you call you a hard worker? Why or why not? Are you taking short cuts? Stop. Work hard at everything you do. Seek excellence.

2. Work for the Lord. Are you leveraging your influence to make Jesus famous? What are your motives in your day-to-day living? Does your drive come from what the world has to offer or what God has to offer? Showing up to practice and working hard should be a result of you being all God has called you to be. The ones who work the hardest rise to the top and have the most influence. God wants you to use that influence to share about Him. Are you working hard to gain influence to make Jesus famous?

3. Don't work to impress. Are you trying to impress man more than you are trying to live for God? "Every man for himself" seems to be the motto of most guys. Sometimes guys lie, cheat, steal, take shortcuts, or do whatever it takes to impress "human masters." We need men who live with character, integrity, and holiness, who at the end of the day know they lived a life that is honoring to their Lord.

DAY 3 MECHANICS OF ATTITUDE

IMAGE

For by the grace given to me I say to everyone among you not to think of himself more highly than he ought to think, but to think with sober judgment, each according to the measure of faith that God has assigned. —Romans 12:3 (ESV)

Unfortunately, we live in a day when a lot of guys are trying to make much of themselves, always feeling the need to one-up the next guy to feel a sense of accomplishment. Whether it is playing sports, lifting weights, or talking to ladies, guys always have a burning need to try to prove themselves.

I remember attempting my first CrossFit workout. The name of the workout is called "Linda." Some in the CrossFit community refer to this workout as "three bars of death." The second name is more fitting. The workout consists of 10 deadlifts at 1.5 times your body weight, 10 bench presses at body weight, and 10 squat cleans at three-fourths your body weight, then you repeat this pattern for nine, eight, seven, and all the way down to one. The only problem was that I never made it. I stopped on my set of six. I was eager to prove myself to those who were doing the workout with me. With a background in sports and lifting weights for almost two hours a day, I thought I was in decent shape. That workout proved otherwise. These movements were not outside of my realm, but there was a small thing called intensity that took me outside my comfort zone.

So why do I mention that story? The reason is that I had a distorted view of myself. I thought I was in decent shape, but that workout proved otherwise.

Too often, we compare ourselves to others and think we are doing pretty well. The Bible warns us how this causes a distorted view of ourselves. (See Rom. 12:3.)

If we think too highly of ourselves, it is likely we devalue others and we don't have a clear understanding of the gospel. Think about it. Just because you have a high view of yourself does not make you any more meaningful than the person next to you. Instead, a person who thinks highly of himself internally devalues others to try to justify his significance. The cure to this problem is viewing the gospel in a clear manner. When we view what Christ accomplished over two thousand years ago, it is very difficult to think highly of ourselves. The reason is that no one or nothing can compare to what He accomplished.

Another way that we distort the view of ourselves is by trying to convince others that we have everything together. This problem is shared by many. When someone asks, "How is your day going?" the natural answer is "great!" Regardless of how we feel or our current struggles, we are taught to hide our difficulties. The Bible teaches us that we as believers are far from perfect. Paul said in Romans 3:23: *All have sinned and fall short of the glory of God.* And we will continue to struggle with our sinful flesh throughout our lives. The hard fact is that we are an imperfect people, living in an imperfect world, but thank God we have a perfect Savior! We have a perfect Savior who accepts our imperfections. He knows we will stumble and fall throughout our journey, and He will always be there to pick us up. Our hope is found in Christ and not in ourselves. This is the beauty of viewing ourselves with the proper lenses. We no longer have to cover up our past or our current failures. Christ loves us, forgives us, and promises to never leave us or forsake us: *And behold, I am with you always, to the end of the age* (Matt. 28:20, ESV). With this in mind, we can admit our imperfections and trust Christ to lead us and guide us as believers.

Ultimately, it is not how we perceive ourselves or how others view us that matters. The only perception that matters is God's. Fortunately we don't stand before God in our own stead. We are clothed in the righteousness of Jesus. His perfection covers our imperfections. There is no need for us to build up our own image. We are covered by Christ! When God looks at us, He sees Jesus.

We can spend our whole lives trying to build ourselves up, or we can simply accept who we are in Christ.

✪ CONSISTENCY ────

1) Follow Christ's example. Jesus wasn't worried about image: *Have this mind among yourselves, which is yours in Christ Jesus, who, though he was in the form of God, did not count equality with God a thing to be grasped, but emptied himself* (Phil. 2:5-7a, ESV). Jesus chose to humble Himself, even though He was the exact radiance of God, He chose to serve instead of be served. Even though He was of infinite worth, He gave Himself for others. This is the example we as believers are called to follow.

2) Don't think too highly of yourself. It is easy to compare ourselves to others and to think more highly of ourselves. Remember, when you think too highly of yourself, you're probably putting others down. Don't devalue the significance of others by putting yourself above them. Apply Paul's words: *Do nothing from selfish ambition or conceit, but in humility count others more significant than yourselves* (Phil. 2:3, ESV).

3) Be honest about who you are. We can be honest about our imperfections. Don't deceive yourself: *If we say we have no sin, we deceive ourselves, and the truth is not in us. If we confess our sins, he is faithful and just to forgive us our sins and to cleanse us from all unrighteousness* (1 John 1:8-9, ESV).

No one is perfect, and God designed us to be dependent upon Him. When we fail, we are reminded that we are in constant need of a Savior. There will never be a time in our walk that we will become independent of God. We can be honest with others along the journey and admit our imperfections.

DAY 4 MECHANICS OF ATTITUDE
RESPONSE

Make your own attitude that of Christ Jesus. —Philippians 2:5 (NLT)

I want to introduce you to Josh Landrith, who in the fall of 2014 started his senior year in high school. Josh is a preacher's kid who I have grown to respect and love dearly. Today I want you to hear a portion of Josh's story:

"Life was always pretty comfortable for me. I never had any real tragedies in my life before. Any news about people being diagnosed with terminal illness or dying in a car wreck or anything like that kind of seemed like it would never happen to me or people in my life. Last March, my father got news from a doctor and all of that changed. He wasn't feeling very good and was having some pains, so he finally went to the doctor about it. They found something that looked slightly suspicious. I remember them telling me that and I thought, 'Okay, but it's probably nothing. Never is.' Turns out, it wasn't nothing. One Thursday night my brother-in-law and sister came in from out of town and we all met in the living room. It was me, my brother, my brother-in-law, my sister, and my parents. My dad told us that he had an extremely rare, very aggressive type of cancer called colorectal melanoma. The average survival time is twenty months, and the maximum is five years. I had no idea what to think. It didn't feel real. I can still tell you pretty much everything about that Thursday, that Friday, and that Sunday when my dad revealed to our church the news. I forgot to mention that my dad is a pastor. A person in our church and community cried with us, prayed for us, was there for us, and loved on us. The body of Christ is a beautiful thing, and it definitely has been revealed to us in these times. It has been a journey. I have been through times since then where I felt peace and confidence in the hope offered by God. There have also been times, though, where

I have felt bitter, anxious, depressed, and angry. If you're dealing with something, don't think you are wrong or not normal because you are experiencing those feelings. Don't think you're not a 'good Christian' because of it. You're just a human like all of us. What matters is not staying there. It is a struggle I face every day. No matter what you are dealing with, though, God loves you. He cares. And what you are facing right now was already planned out in His mind for a greater purpose before the universe was spoken into being by Him. I believe in the God that raised Lazarus from the dead, but I also believe in the same God who allowed the Devil to torment Job. Both of those stories brought glory to God, though. What matters with your story and your struggles is that it brings glory to God. That hinges on your obedience and your trust in Him. It is not easy. It is not something you can do by yourself. And trials are not just tragic things in life. Some people struggle with depression, anxiety, and anger and have not experienced something like this. Your problems and struggles are not less important than mine or anyone else who has had harder circumstances in life. If you need help for your issues, get help. There is no shame in that, and it does not mean you're weak. It means you are strong enough to take the steps to get yourself the help you need, and to help you figure things out. I believe God could heal my dad and I pray for that. I also believe that He might not, but I understand that ultimately what happens will be for His glory and for a purpose that a mere man like myself cannot understand. Trust God in whatever you are going through, and don't think that you have to go through whatever you're facing alone. There are people who love you and want to help you."

Josh's focus on Christ dictates his response. How we view Christ determines how we respond to any situation in our lives. Does your attitude reflect Christ or the world? When life gets hard, and it will at times, your attitude will reflect what you have been pouring into your life. Life will not always go your way, but Christ will always be with you.

 CONSISTENCY ————

1. Evaluate your attitude. Are you totally trusting Christ and walking with Him daily? How does that affect your attitude? Evaluate your life today and determine if you are filling your life with Christ or the world. Turn your focus to Jesus, so that when faced with whatever life throws at you, you can have an attitude of joy and peace found only in Him.

2. Take time today to confess to God your attitude. We all have moments in which we have a bad attitude. Life is hard and sometimes it gets the best of us. Take your struggling attitude to Jesus. Lay it before Him and ask Him to change your heart to trust Him no matter what.

3. Take action. What needs to change in your life so that your attitude reflects Christ? It could be a decision you've put off, a sin you need to confess, or a relationship you need to get out of. What is it for you? Take action today.

DAY 5 MECHANICS OF ATTITUDE
AWARENESS

Not that I am speaking of being in need, for I have learned in whatever situation I am to be content. —Philippians 4:11 (ESV)

Awareness allows us to see the many blessings that we have in our lives. All of us experience the blessings of God. Whether it is family, friends, health, or just the air we breathe, we all have something or someone to be thankful for. The problem many of us face is realizing those blessings. We tend to focus on what we don't have instead of what we do. Perspective is everything, and the way we view our lives is a reflection of our thankfulness toward God. Let's look at a couple of examples of people who we believed to have it all.

If you are familiar with Michael Jordan, you would know that he is viewed as the greatest basketball player of all time. He won six championships with the Chicago Bulls, and many viewed him as untouchable on the basketball court. Off the court, he signed a huge contract with Nike® and they released his own tennis shoe brand (Jordan). Many would look at Michael's life and wish they were in his shoes. However, Michael never lost the passion of wanting to be on the court. Even though he had retired, he came out of retirement to play a couple of years with the Washington Wizards. Michael was often not content, and he struggled with looking toward the things he didn't have rather than things he already had.

That story stresses the importance of how we view our lives and the blessings we have been given. There is no doubt that Michael Jordan achieved amazing things throughout his basketball career. However, championships, money, and fame alone cannot bring eternal contentment. The only thing in this lifetime that can bring eternal contentment is a proper view and response to the gospel.

When we truly grasp the gospel, we realize how blessed we are as believers. We understand that no matter what we may or may not have in this lifetime, we have Jesus Christ and all the spiritual blessings that come from being a child of God, including being with Him forever.

That is what Paul was talking about when he wrote in Philippians 4:12: *I have learned the secret of being content.* Everlasting contentment is not determined by gaining more stuff. Instead, everlasting contentment is found only in what God has already freely given us. Whether it is big or small blessings, we need to learn to give thanks to God for everything in our lives: *Give thanks in all circumstances; for this is the will of God in Christ Jesus for you* (1 Thess. 5:18, ESV).

Awareness allows us to rejoice in the small things instead of creating an endless pursuit in chasing the big things. No doubt it would be nice to be in the shoes of Michael Jordan. He has a lot to be thankful for. However, without a clear view of the gospel, we would never be satisfied. That is the beauty of being a believer. Believers know that they can rejoice in any and every circumstance. For they know that regardless of being rich or poor, successful or struggling, popular or unknown, they can still find contentment in Christ.

Awareness brings any difficult situation into a learning opportunity: *Count it all joy, my brothers, when you meet trials of various kinds, for you know that the testing of your faith produces steadfastness. And let steadfastness have its full effect, that you may be perfect and complete, lacking in nothing* (Jas. 1:2-4, ESV).

Awareness also brings any blessing God gives us into a rejoicing opportunity. However, without awareness it will be difficult to view our current position with the proper lens. Only through the gospel and having a clear view of our position in Christ can we view any and all circumstances as an opportunity to rejoice and make much of Christ. With awareness, we can echo the cry of Paul that we too have learned how to be content in any and every situation.

CONSISTENCY ————

1) Raise awareness through the Word. Spending time in God's Word changes your perspective. The more you immerse yourself in the Word, the better you understand all God is and all you have to be thankful for. Build your awareness of blessings by valuing God's Word: *For a day in your courts is better than a thousand elsewhere. I would rather be a doorkeeper in the house of my God than dwell in the tents of wickedness. For the LORD God is a sun and shield; the LORD bestows favor and honor. No good thing does he withhold from those who walk uprightly* (Ps. 84:10-11, ESV).

2) Focus on what you have. Spend 10 minutes today focusing on what God has given you instead of what you perceive to not have. List your blessings and pray with thanksgiving through your list. Some areas to focus on: spiritual blessings, family, friends, provisions (food, shelter, transportation), health, and anything else that we may take for granted. No matter how small or insignificant it may seem, write it down and give thanks for it. Also spend time thanking God for the difficult things you are going through. Thank Him for His presence and purpose and what He's teaching you. Follow this command: *Rejoice always, pray without ceasing, give thanks in all circumstances; for this is the will of God in Christ Jesus for you* (1 Thess. 5:16-18, ESV).

DAY 6 MECHANICS OF ATTITUDE
INTENSITY

This week you have been challenged to have an attitude like that of Christ Jesus. Attitudes come from within. What you put in will determine what you put out.

Great athletes and leaders miss out on great opportunities because they never commit to the cause ahead of them. Because they have wrong expectations or feel entitled, they don't work as hard. The entitled attitude keeps many from being great. We need more guys who have the attitude of Christ Jesus no matter the circumstance.

We need a clear understanding of the cause we are fighting for. Paul fought the good fight of faith (2 Tim. 4:7). He did not waver in living for the cause of Christ. Nothing was more important to Him. Philippians 1:21 says: *For to me to live is Christ, and to die is gain* (ESV). Paul's mission was to share the gospel. He remained faithful to that call from God regardless of the circumstances. We must do he same. I love how John MacArthur in his book *Called to Lead* describes Jesus' attitude in picking His disciples: "In Christ's day the world was filled with intellectuals and influential people. There were celebrated philosophers in Athens, unsurpassed scholars in Alexandria, the most powerful political leaders the world had ever known in Rome, and some of the most meticulous rabbis of all time in and around Jerusalem. Christ bypassed them all and called simple, crude, unknown, and uneducated fisherman from Galilee to be His disciples."[26] Christ was not sent to please this world but to impact this world.

The challenge for you this week is to have that type of attitude. The attitude that says, "I will go for it and never waver from my faith. I will never let the world determine who I am and who I follow." We need men who are 100 percent committed to the cause of Christ and are willing to do whatever it takes to take the gospel around the world.

Day 1: Mechanics of Attitude – Motivation (Col. 3:17)

1. What motivates you the most?
2. Are you spiritually motivated to follow God's call on your life? Why or why not?
3. What do you want to be remembered for? Do you value leaving a spiritual legacy? Explain.

Day 2: Mechanics of Attitude – Hard Work (Col. 3:23)

1. What areas in your life do you see yourself taking shortcuts?
2. Do you grasp the concept that you are working for God and not for human accolades? Explain.
3. How does the phrase "work at it with all your heart" apply to your day-to-day life? How does your work ethic reflect your faith?

Day 3: Mechanics of Attitude – Image (Rom. 12:3)

1. Why do guys get so focused on their image?
2. How do you see the comparison trap affecting your friends and yourself?
3. Why are guys not more honest about who they really are? What steps do you need to take to be real about who you are?

Day 4: Mechanics of Attitude – Response (Phil. 2:5)

1. How do you respond to difficult situations?
2. What Scriptures bring comfort and focus when the storms of life hit?
3. Does your life reflect the attitude of Christ? Explain.

Day 5: Mechanics of Attitude – Awareness (Phil. 4:11)

1. What blessings in your life do you tend to overlook?
2. What in life are you chasing the most? Is it bringing satisfaction? Explain.
3. Are you struggling with being content? Explain. What needs to change for you to find total contentment in Christ?

NOTES

NOTES

SOURCES

1. Greg Glassman, "Virtuosity," *Crossfit Journal* [online], [cited 7 November 2014]. Available from the Internet: *http://journal.crossfit.com/2005/08/virtuosity-1.tpl*

2. C.J. Mahaney, *Humility: True Greatness* (Sisters, OR: Mulnomah Books, 2005), 22.

3. "'Spoiled' Cheerleader, 18, Who Sued Parents for Child Support Agrees to Dismiss Lawsuit," *Daily Mail* [online], 18 March 2014 [cited 7 November 2014]. Available from the Internet: *www.dailymail.co.uk/news/article-2583590/Spoiled-cheerleader-18-sued-parents-child-support-agrees-dismiss-lawsuit.html#ixzz3HjOSSgzr*

4. Rick Reilly, "The Patience of Jim," *ESPN* [online], 4 March 2012 [cited 7 November 2014]. Available from the Internet: *http://espn.go.com/nfl/story/_/id/10549870/former-buffalo-bills-quarterback-jim-kelly-patiently-endures-cancer-loss*

5. *Search Quotes* [online], [cited 7 November 2014]. Available from the Internet: *www.searchquotes.com/search/I_Know_That_The_Hard_Work_Got_Me_Here_And_The/*

6. Denver Nicks, "ESPN Draws Fire Over Reporter's Reaction to Kevin Durant Thanking God," 30 January 2014 [cited 7 November 2014]. Available from the Internet: *http://time.com/3145/espn-draws-fire-over-reporters-reaction-to-kevin-durant-thanking-god/*

7. Jon McArthur, *Galatians: The MacArthur New Testament Commentary*, (Chicago, IL: Moody Publishers, 1987), 60.

8. Rodolfo F. Acuna, *When Do You Start Counting?* (Carol Stream, IL: NavPress, 2006).

9. Jerry Bridges, "The Fruitful Life," (Carol Stream, IL: NavPress, 2006).

10. Richard Allen, "Michael Phelps Workout and Diet, *Muscle Prodigy* [online], 11 December 2011 [cited 10 November 2014].

11. Laura Lee Cole, "Never Complacent," 12 July 2014 [cited 7 November 2014]. Available from the Internet: *http://games.crossfit.com/article/never-complacent*

12. "Theodore Roosevelt Quotes," *Wisdom Quotes* [online], [cited 7 November 2014]. Available from the Internet: *www.wisdomquotes.com/quote/theodore-roosevelt-2.html*

13. O.S. Hawkins, *The Joshua Code: 52 Scripture Verses Every Believer Should Know*, (Nashville, TN: Thomas Nelson, 2012).

SOURCES

14. Trent Butler, *Holman Old testament Commentary – Isaiah,* (Nashville, TN: Broadman & Holman, 2002).

15. David Mathis, "Sanctification: So Why the Long Word?" *Desiring God* [online], 4 August 2012 [cited 7 November 2014]. Available from the Internet: *www.desir"inggod.org/blog/posts/sanctification-so-why-the-long-word*

16. John Maxwell, *The 21 Irrefutable Laws of Leadership,* (Nashville: Thomas Nelson, 2005), 14.

17. J.A. Witmer, Witmer, J. A. (1985). Romans. In J. F. Walvoord & R. B. Zuck (Eds.), The Bible Knowledge Commentary: An Exposition of the Scriptures (Vol. 2, p. 476). Wheaton, IL: Victor Books. (this is 5, commitment)

18. Eugene Allen, "Killer Workouts," [cited 7 November 2014]. Available from the Internet: *www.crossfit.com/journal/library/33_05_killer_workouts.pdf*

19. Timothy Keller, "Counterfeit Gods," (New York, NY: Penguin Group, 2009).

20. Becky Barrow, "How the cost of living and the working week has changed over 60 years: Flexible hours and more time off now... but we're no happier," *This is Money,* 1 February 2012 [cited 7 Novemeber 2014]. Available from the Internet: *www.thisismoney.co.uk/money/news/article-2094850/How-working-week-changed-60-years--CIPD.html*

21. Brian Mills and Nathan Wagnon, *Checkpoints - A Tactical Guide to Manhood* (Carol Stream, IL: NavPress, 2012), 98.

22. Nepoleon, "Nepoleon's Argument for the Divinity of Christ and the Scriptures" (Charleston: The South Carolina Tract Society, 2012), 1-2.

23. K.A. Richardson, "James" (Vol. 36), (Nashville: Broadman & Holman Publishers, 1997), 89.

24. T.D. Lea, "Hebrews, James" (Vol. 10), (Nashville, TN: Broadman & Holman Publishers, 1999), 264.

25. J.S. Deere, "Deuteronomy" (Vol. 1), (Wheaton, IL: Victor Books, 1985), 316.

26. John MacArther, *Called to Lead* (Nashville, TN: Thomas Nelson, 2010), 151.